Cambridge Elements

Elements in Public and Nonprofit Administration
edited by
Andrew Whitford
University of Georgia
Robert Christensen
Brigham Young University

EXPERTS IN GOVERNMENT

The Deep State from Caligula to Trump and Beyond

Donald F. Kettl
University of Maryland

CAMBRIDGE
UNIVERSITY PRESS

Shaftesbury Road, Cambridge CB2 8EA, United Kingdom

One Liberty Plaza, 20th Floor, New York, NY 10006, USA

477 Williamstown Road, Port Melbourne, VIC 3207, Australia

314–321, 3rd Floor, Plot 3, Splendor Forum, Jasola District Centre,
New Delhi – 110025, India

103 Penang Road, #05–06/07, Visioncrest Commercial, Singapore 238467

Cambridge University Press is part of Cambridge University Press & Assessment,
a department of the University of Cambridge.

We share the University's mission to contribute to society through the pursuit of
education, learning and research at the highest international levels of excellence.

www.cambridge.org
Information on this title: www.cambridge.org/9781009478625

DOI: 10.1017/9781009276085

First published 2023

A catalogue record for this publication is available from the British Library

ISBN 978-1-009-47862-5 Hardback
ISBN 978-1-009-27610-8 Paperback
ISSN 2515-4303 (online)
ISSN 2515-429X (print)

Cambridge University Press & Assessment has no responsibility for the persistence
or accuracy of URLs for external or third-party internet websites referred to in this
publication and does not guarantee that any content on such websites is, or will
remain, accurate or appropriate.

Experts in Government

The Deep State from Caligula to Trump and Beyond

Elements in Public and Nonprofit Administration

DOI: 10.1017/9781009276085
First published online: December 2023

Donald F. Kettl
University of Maryland
Author for correspondence: Donald F. Kettl, dfkettl52@gmail.com

Abstract: From Caligula and the time of ancient Rome to the present, governments have relied on experts to manage public programs. But with that expertise has come power, and that power has long proven difficult to hold accountable. The tension between experts in the bureaucracy and the policy goals of elected officials, however, remains a point of often bitter tension. President Donald Trump labeled these experts as a "deep state" seeking to resist the policies he believed he was elected to pursue – and he developed a policy scheme to make it far easier to fire experts he deemed insufficiently loyal. The age-old battles between expertise and accountability have come to a sharp point, and resolving these tensions requires a fresh look at the rule of law to shape the role of experts in governance.

This Element also has a video abstract: www.cambridge.org/Kettl

Keywords: "deep state," experts, civil service, constitution, rule of law

ISBNs: 9781009478625 (HB), 9781009276108 (PB), 9781009276085 (OC)
ISSNs: 2515-4303 (online), 2515-429X (print)

Contents

1 Paradoxes

The fundamental, eternal paradox about experts in government is this: it is impossible to implement complicated government programs, from roads to national defense, without experts. However, expert knowledge inevitably creates its own political power and instability, because it is always hard for government leaders to know enough to keep that power in check. Leaders need experts, and they expect them to be loyal. Leaders also want loyalists, and they expect them to be experts. That creates an eternally uneasy quest for balance. As we shall see, from Caligula to Trump and beyond, that is the central challenge of governance.

The bureaucracy houses the government's experts, but there is another paradox here. These bureaucracies often appear both so powerful as to be impossible to control – but so impotent as to stumble in delivering the programs that people count on. It is hard to remember that bureaucratic power was created to accomplish the government's mission, not the other way around. Nor was it created to generate jobs for loyalists or to protect the jobs of those already employed.

Relying on experts, however, has always brought its risks. Caligula's own Praetorian Guard, a force of Rome's best-trained soldiers whose primary job was to protect the emperor, assassinated him in 41 CE, because they disagreed with his accumulation of power and feared he was becoming increasingly unstable. (Some writers at the time reported that he planned to make his horse Incitatus a consul of Rome, although historians tend to agree that the stallion never sat in the Senate.) There is no better manifestation of the risks of the "deep state" than the fact that the Roman "deep state" turned on the very emperor who helped feed it.

In modern times, there is a growing complaint that government jobs in the civil service have created a "creeping concentration of power in administrative agencies, where much of that power has been handed to a career civil service that is increasingly distant from political accountability," as former Trump administration official David L. Bernhardt (2023, 209) put it. To direct and at least try to control these bureaucracies, we have created a vast collection of procedures, but enforcing these procedures often become ends in themselves – a "procedure fetish," as Nicholas Bagley (2019) calls it, a fetish that has bogged down public management. The mission of public programs often gets lost in the morass of ritual and rule and culture.

There is also the complaint that the bureaucracy has become a power unto itself. As Bernhardt (2023) continues, career administrators "are not in government to be policy zealots untethered by law." This complaint became known simply as the "deep state," a system devoted to serving itself instead of the policies of elected officials and derived from the Turkish government's collusion with the military in the 1990s to suppress Kurdish insurgents (Worth 2017).

Donald Trump's successful 2016 campaign for the presidency picked up on the theme of a large, hidden, and uncontrolled bureaucracy and used it to chart his approach to governance. Indeed, just days after the inauguration in 2017, adviser Stephen Bannon pledged a "deconstruction of the administrative state." In complaining about the permanent bureaucracy not long after Trump's inauguration in 2017, Bannon said, "If you think they're going to give you your country back without a fight, you are sadly mistaken. . . . Every day, it is going to be a fight" (Rucker and Costa 2017). And as the president rolled out new policies, he and his top advisers were convinced that the bureaucracy was blockading his policies. As described in a 2018 *New York Times* op-ed, bylined by "Anonymous" and later confirmed by the *Times* as written by Miles Taylor, chief of staff in the Department of Homeland Security, "many of the senior officials in his own administration are working diligently from within to frustrate parts of his agenda and his worst inclinations." Taylor continued, "I would know. I am one of them" (Anonymous 2018). Trump became convinced that the "deep state" was a reality.

Not everyone, of course, agreed with the assault on the government's career experts. A team of researchers, for example, conducted a meta-analysis of ninety-six articles about civil service systems around the world. They found that weakening the civil service "likely decreases government performance and increases corruption" (Oliveira et al. 2023, 20). But this tension – between the power of experts and the struggle of top officials to control them – has become the cutting edge of debates about the future of the American government. As we will see in the pages that follow, its roots and challenges reach back to the very beginnings of bureaucracy in ancient times.

The Historical Roots of the Rule of Law

For much of history, especially since the days of the Roman and Chinese empires, there has been an ongoing struggle to enhance the government's *capacity* – enhancing the bureaucracy that the government needed to accomplish its mission – while strengthening the government's *control* over the bureaucracy. That story, as I will show in the sections that follow, is one in which experts worked to craft a rule of law to steady a balance between capacity and control.

The foundations of the rule of law to find that balance date from Hammurabi, who ruled Babylon from 1792 to 1750 BCE. His code of 282 rules laid out guidelines for everything from commercial transactions to punishments for those who violated the kingdom's system of justice. It laid out legal precedents, some of which were quite severe. A doctor might be paid royally for curing a severe wound or illness, but if a doctor's intervention killed a well-to-do patient, he would be unable to further practice medicine because his hands would have been cut off. At the core, Hammurabi's code sought "to prevent the strong from oppressing the weak and to see that justice is done to widows and orphans" (Cormacain 2022, 269). One item in Hammurabi's code sets a far tougher standard for a court's role than anyone would imagine for the present:

> If a judge try a case, reach a decision, and present his judgment in writing; if later error shall appear in his decision, and it be through his own fault, then he shall pay twelve times the fine set by him in the case, and he shall be publicly removed from the judge's bench, and never again shall he sit there to render judgment. (King, n.d.)

Civilization has long been built on the rule of law. And nothing is more important in the rule of law than to set the balance between the government's experts and the need to control their exercise of authority.

Bureaucratic Experts and the Proxy War between Government's Size and Power

Over two millennia, the quest for a rule of law to create and control government bureaucracy has been perhaps the central issue of governance. There has never been a stable answer for long but, especially in the United States and particularly since the 1980s, the bureaucracy became less an instrument to accomplish the government's goals and more a symbol of the government's size, wealth, and power. Republicans attacked programs they did not like by attacking the bureaucracy and undermining the government's capacity to manage them. That is the core of Bannon's attack. Democrats developed ambitious policy ideas but frequently paid little attention to the bureaucratic institutions required to produce results. It is no coincidence that the academic movement to examine implementation, including the book by Jeffrey L. Pressman and Aaron Wildavsky with the classic subtitle that wondered, in part, "why it's amazing that federal programs work at all," grew out of the disappointment with the Democrats' War on Poverty in the 1960s (Pressman and Wildavsky 1973).

In fact, the debate over the government bureaucracy has become a proxy war over the government's size and power. It is not just a question of just how strong or dangerous the government bureaucracy ought to be. It is an even more fundamental debate about the very essence of government itself. And it is a debate that stretches back 2,000 years.

In the sections that follow, I will explain how, since ancient times, the rule of law has grown into an instrument to shape and control bureaucratic power. I will then show how that long-term development fizzled in the face of more-recent ideological battles over the government's size and purpose. From ideologically driven privatization to personnel cuts to attacks on the very constitutionality of the government's system for filling jobs, the debate about the role of government bureaucracy and the experts within it has never been more contentious.

Finally, I will lay out ideas about how to solve this problem. The solutions will focus both at the micro level – how best to untangle the proceduralism that has crippled the public service – and at the macro level – how to focus the political system on the connection between the results it seeks and the tools it needs to do so. In the end, though, the central issue rises to the top. The role of experts is not fundamentally technical. Devising the best strategy for setting that role is fundamentally political, and any effort to deal with these issues must end as it begins, with a frank recognition of the political power that technical experts wield.

Many of these issues apply as well to other governance systems in the twenty-first century. But most of my story will focus on the perils of the American government, which has found itself buried in the paradox of governance – by the inability to grapple with the twin goals of competence and control.

This is the fundamental puzzle of this Element: how can we make bureaucracy strong enough to accomplish the goals that policymakers assign to it, without making it so strong that it undermines the power of top officials – and, in democracies, the liberty of individuals?

2 Power

No state can function long without experts, and these experts invariably create an independent source of power. As the famous sociologist Max Weber (1947, 339) wrote, "bureaucratic administration means fundamentally the exercise of control on the basis of knowledge. "That knowledge, in turn, inevitably leads to political power, and political power in the hands of administrators creates problems of control (Bendix 1945). It is an eternal issue replayed constantly across the ages. The more ambitious that government gets, the more it depends on experts. The larger the role of experts, the more worries about their power grow. And the more those worries grow, the greater the political conflict around the experts and the bureaucracies that house them. Before moving to how this puzzle evolved over the years, however, let me tell two tales about these underlying tensions: about control, through Donald Trump's complaints about reining in the "deep state"; and about competence, through the city of Austin's struggles with its water system.

Trump and Control

From his administration's first days, Trump complained that the permanent bureaucracy undermined his presidency. When reporters questioned Trump press secretary Sean Spicer about whether there was a "deep state" working to undermine the president, Spicer replied, "Well, I think that there's no question, when you have eight years of one party in office, that there are people who stay in government who are affiliated with – you know, join and continue to espouse the agenda of the previous administration" (Schwartz 2017). By the end of his administration, 39 percent of Americans concluded there was a "deep state" working to undermine Trump (IPSOS 2020).

The "deep state" argument focused especially on public health experts who, the president believed, were intent on undermining the economy as well as his reelection. The ongoing attacks undermined the experts' advice on the COVID-19 outbreak in 2020. Adults from the United States who said they had a "great deal" of confidence in medical experts dropped sharply from 40 percent in November 2020 to 29 percent in February 2022. The view of Republicans toward public health officials was much lower (29 percent) than for Democrats (72 percent).

In March 2020, 66 percent of Americans said that the virus was a "major threat" to public health. In May 2022, that dropped to 41 percent, thanks in part to the growing availability of the vaccine, which reduced the spread of the disease. But despite the progress against COVID-19, critics called for the arrest of Dr. Anthony Fauci, the nation's premier infectious disease specialist, whom they claimed had lied about support for Chinese labs, which they believed had been the source of the virus. Some Republican presidential candidates in the run-up to the 2024 presidential election said they would have supported firing Fauci.

Toward the end of the Trump administration, a senior policy adviser, James Sherk, argued that the "intransigence" of federal bureaucrats, who were "deeply partisan" and opposed Trump and his policies, "effectively cancels Americans' ballots by blocking policies their elected officials voted for" (Sherk 2022a). He contended that "too often, insubordinate employees subvert the work of political appointees" put in their positions by the president. Many times, he complained, he found "career staff undermining presidential policies." The resistance of career experts "significantly delayed many policy initiatives and killed others" through "sabotage" (Sherk 2022b).

Sherk logged complaints about careerists who "exercise federal power without adequate transparency and democratic accountability." He pointed to career attorneys in the Civil Rights Division of the Department of Justice who, he said, refused to prosecute cases with which they ideologically disagreed and career attorneys in the Environmental Protection Agency who did not inform their political superiors about pending cases (Sherk 2022b). In preparing the Heritage Foundation's playbook on the bureaucracy for the 2024 election, Donald Devine, Dennis Dean Kirk, and Paul Dans supported Sherk's point. They wrote, "The specific deficiencies of the federal bureaucracy – size, levels of organization, inefficiency, expense, and lack of responsiveness to political leadership – are rooted in the progressive ideology that unelected experts can and should be trusted to promote the general welfare in just about every area of social life" (Devine, Kirk, and Dans 2023, 83).

Reporters found that careerists throughout the government were in fact quietly working to undermine the policies developed by the president and his appointees. There actually was a "deep state" – at least to the degree of slow-walking the president's policies, including those on COVID-19, and continuing the policies of the Obama administration, such as climate change (Flavelle and Bain 2017). But the larger question was whether the problem lay in how Trump's administrators overstepped their bounds or how the career bureaucracy proved intransigent.

The "deep state" complaints stretched across the globe. One cynic tweeted in 2021, "Most democracies are run by a nameless, faceless bureaucracy" (Naval 2021). The image of a nameless, faceless, powerful, permanent bureaucracy is an enduring icon in the critique of government's power. Analysts pointed to the "nameless, faceless bureaucracy" in India (Singhvi 2014). British prime minister Boris Johnson claimed that a "deep state" was trying to drag the nation back into an alliance with the European Union, with the "deep state" filling the offices of the European Commission's bureaucracy in Brussels (Elledge 2022). Conspiracy theories spilled across the ocean to Japan (Zimmerman 2020), and Brazilian president Jair Bolsonaro proved so successful in promoting the theme that he had become known as the "Trump of the Tropics" (Roberts 2019).

Some of the charges against the "deep state" were often exaggerated or frequently outlandish. For example, some of the complaints came from followers of QAnon, a conservative fringe group whose members believed that Democrats and leading journalists ate babies and drank children's blood. However, at least some experts, buried deep in the government bureaucracy, undoubtedly slow-walked or even undermined policies with which they disagreed. Behind the scenes, many experienced government leaders have their own tales of trying to deal with troublemaking employees.

At the core, the "deep state" debate was about the power of the bureaucracy, based on its expertise, and the problems that power raised for elected officials and their senior appointees. For the officials complaining about the "deep state," the bureaucratic experts were a constant source of frustration. Trump allies, like Sen. Lindsey Graham (R-SC), were fond of pointing out that "elections have consequences" (Graham 2022). Their frustration was that they believed that the permanent bureaucracy tried to undermine their policies and power.

So, when it came to finding a balance between bureaucratic control and capacity, they leaned heavily to control. Ensuring accountability for the bureaucracy's exercise of its expertise was, for those who worried about the "deep state," far more important than exercising the bureaucracy's capacity.

But in Austin, residents suffered when the city's administrative capacity was not strong enough.

Austin and Competence

Austin, Texas has always prided itself on being a bit kitschy, with the slogan "Keep Austin Weird" emblazoned on t-shirts, along with souvenir mugs celebrating the city's urban bat colony. But it has also prided itself on a city government with a high level of professionalism. Its popularity soared during the 2010s, drawing many new residents from California's tech sector to the city's easy culture and lower cost of living. That population growth – more than 20 percent during the decade – put severe pressure on much of the city's infrastructure. Austin's water system had particularly suffered under the strain, with three boil-water notices in just four years. During the same period, San Antonio, a city 40 percent larger, had none.

The February 2022 collapse of Austin's water system was especially embarrassing. On a Friday evening, the operators of one of the city's water treatment plants were performing maintenance. By Saturday morning, the operators noticed a marked increase in "turbidity," or the cloudiness of the water, and they worried that was a sign that impurities could leak into the system. The system's managers immediately sent out a warning to all the system's customers, telling users that they needed to boil their water before drinking it. They issued a terse statement pointing to "errors from our operating staff" (Sandoval and Goodman 2022).

Six weeks later, the city completed a damning assessment of what had happened. Austin Water director Greg Meszaros explained, "This in-depth investigatory process has confirmed our preliminary findings that there were failures in staff's response to deteriorating plant conditions and communications up the chain of command." He added, "This is unacceptable, and Austin Water managers are taking steps to ensure that it does not happen again" (Austin Water 2022a).

A water basin had been taken out of service for repairs, and three employees were on duty to bring it back online. They added calcium carbonate – lime – to reduce the acidity of the water flowing in from the city's water source the Colorado River. But the operators added too much of the chemical for too long. Instead of putting it into the system for a few hours on Friday evening, they allowed it to continue to flow overnight and they missed the alarms warning of the error until 8:00 a.m. the next morning. The mistake increased the cloudiness of the water (McGlinchy 2022).

The operators did not inform their supervisors about the problem and the cloudiness of the water worsened. Top officials did not want to take any chances and sent out word on Saturday morning to boil their water before drinking it. A few days later, the director of Austin Water sent out a profound apology: "We have heard directly from you and our residents. Residents are angry, frustrated, and have lost trust in us. I share your frustration and am deeply disappointed that this event occurred. Knowing how it has affected this community and our organization weighs heavily on me." It took twelve hours from the occurrence of the error to begin notifying customers. Errors in the notification system meant that some customers did not find out about the problem until six hours later than others. It was an enormous embarrassment for Austin Water. Austin residents were furious about having to boil their water for the third time in the previous four years. And then, to cap the frustration, a later investigation revealed that there had been no need to boil the water to begin with. It had been safe to drink all along.

It was easy to blame the three operators for the problem. They had in fact made horrendous mistakes: not tracking their work to prepare the tank, not noticing the alarms, and not notifying supervisors. But there was a larger problem. Austin Water had a vacancy rate of 11 percent among its employees, and the utility had lost twenty employees in January alone, including operators with decades of experience (Autullo 2022). In short, the city's water system, serving more than a million residents, broke down because of the lack of administrative capacity. The operator on duty, the city's final report concluded, "failed to perform the duties of his position at a level of cooperation, efficiency, and economy acceptable to Austin Water and the City" (Austin Water 2022b).

The Dilemma of Control and Capacity

These two cases frame the issues of control and capacity. Trump and his team charged the permanent bureaucracy with being out of control – or, at least, out of their control, as elected officials. Austin residents suffered at the hands of an agency that lacked the capacity to manage its water system well. The Centre for Public Impact (2016) concluded that this was truly a global problem:

> No matter where one lives, making government deliver effectively for its citizens is one of the great moral issues of our time.
>
> But when most political leaders arrive in office, they find that delivering results is the hardest part of the job. Formally speaking, they have authority to direct what government does. But they sit on top of a large and complicated bureaucracy, and it's not immediately evident how to work through it to get things done. At the same time, political leaders must of course manage politics – the inevitable day-to-day distractions of events that public figures must deal with.
>
> The challenge feels intractable.

There is a long theoretical tradition along this line of argument, starting with Pressman and Wildavsky's *Implementation*. But even Winston Churchill weighed in. In a letter he wrote to the author H. G. Wells, he said, "Nothing would be more fatal than for the Government of States to get in the hands of experts" (Churchill 1902), though his tongue seemed planted firmly in his cheek. But worries about the misguided power of experts have been an ongoing and irresistible target. Conservative writer William F. Buckley said, "I'd rather entrust the government of the United States to the first 2,000 people in the telephone directory than by the Harvard University faculty" (Wakefield 1961).

As long as there have been civilizations, there have been government experts to build and rule them. As long as there have been experts in government, the experts have cultivated power. And if bureaucrats have had power, it has been difficult to control them. The more they are controlled, the harder it is to attract experts.

Control of bureaucratic expertise through the rule of law, on one side, and the risks to the rule of law by powerful bureaucrats, on the other, is the core puzzle of governmental power. Indeed, as Christopher Hood (1998) pointed out, bureaucratic control is at the core of the art of the state. That has been the case for thousands of years.

In the twenty-first century, however, the challenges of bureaucratic capacity and control became far greater. When it comes to capacity, the delivery of public programs has become more complex, stretching across multiple organizations without a single point of management (Eggers and Kettl 2023). And when it comes to control, the multiplication of organizations involved in implementation and the growing complexity of programs makes it difficult for policy-makers and the people to find leverage over the administrative system.

This puzzle is ageless. It has never been possible to have governance without bureaucracy, and every bureaucracy poses the twin puzzle of control and capacity. But this puzzle is also growing, with deeper implications for how societies seek to resolve it.

In the sections that follow, I will explore the historical roots and modern challenges of this tradeoff, through a series of historical stages:

- Law: the creation of governance through a rule of law, as shaped both by the ancient Chinese and Roman systems of government.
- Knowledge: the experts who provided the light through the Dark Ages.
- Institutions: the expansion of government's role in society through the creation of powerful institutions.
- Ripening: the evolution of these institutions into the modern age.
- Sclerosis: the hardening of the governance arteries through intractable tensions between capacity and control.

In the Element's last two sections, I will examine the more recent tensions that have developed in the United States between the issues of capacity and control.

- Mission: the struggle to shift the bureaucracy from a preoccupation with process to a focus on accomplishing the government's goals.
- Accountability: the options for solving the ultimate challenge of bureaucracy – how, once it gains the capacity to focus on its mission, its work can be held accountable in the increasingly complex world of twenty-first century governance.

But first, in Section 3, I will turn to the foundations of bureaucracy in the rule of law, as developed in ancient China and Rome.

3 Law

For ancient China and Rome, the challenge of capacity and control was a two-part problem: finding the experts that the government needed and creating a rule of law to control the use of their power. That effort begins with the strategy of China's ancient emperors, and their basic strategies endure. When visiting China, in fact, I was always struck by the esteem in which society held scholars, widely revered for ages as its experts. In digging deeper, I discovered that, around 960 BCE, Chinese scholars had porters who carried them from meeting to meeting in sedan chairs. If that practice were adopted today in the United States, faculty meetings would certainly take on a completely different air. But the sedan chairs signaled a fundamental truth about Chinese life a millennium ago. Experts enjoyed remarkable status and trust. Chinese governance depended on experts and, millennia ago, its leaders reinforced their power and enhanced their programs by framing the role of civil servants, as we now call them.

As Francis Fukuyama pointed out, "successful liberal democracy requires both a state that is strong, unified, and able to enforce laws on its own territory, and a society that is strong and cohesive and able to impose accountability on the state. It is the balance between a strong state and a strong society that makes democracy work" (Fukuyama 2011, 479). Creating a state with sufficient capacity to govern while not so strong as to threaten the power of leaders is the central challenge for government, in both ancient and modern times, for it is the fundamental problem of public administration.

The Chinese Roots of Bureaucracy

It is not surprising, therefore, that enforcing laws drove the work of many early leaders. Experts were essential to these societies, and the leaders who were most expert were military leaders who succeeded in building the force needed to protect their power. Much of the Bible revolves around armed conquest, both on behalf of and at the expense of the Israelites. Alexander the Great was great because of his military prowess. Pharaohs were powerful not only because of their bridge between man and the gods but also because of their military success. That was especially the case for the Egyptian pharaoh Thutmose III, who won more battles than either Alexander or Julius Caesar (Gabriel 2009).

In the east, the success of the Qin dynasty in conquering other warring states led to the first effective rule of China. The dynasty's most prominent ruler, Shang Yang, created a pyramidal system of government, with groups of families overseen by a collection of counties, and the counties coordinated by the ruler. The system of government had its roots in the military. Indeed, the dynasty is perhaps best known today for its incredible Terracotta Army, with thousands of life-size warriors supported by terra-cotta horses created to defend the emperor in his afterlife. Through the governance pyramid, Li Feng (2013, 239) reports, "the Qin state was thoroughly bureaucratized."

The Qin dynasty created a system of property taxes, along with a sophisticated system of keeping family size small so that the head of a family could not combine all the family's property to escape its tax burden. The government created standard units of length, weight, and volume, and it built a new capital city to serve as the center of the government's future power. Shang Yang's policies and power, in turn, brought down the crime rate, along a path "that aimed at strengthening the economic foundation of the state and promoted the rule of law" (Li 2013, 240).

Shang Yang's revolutionary changes enraged many of the old, established powers. When his patron Duke Xiao died in 338 BCE, those powers pushed him aside. Their army quickly routed his small force and, as Li tells, he was "captured for execution with five chariots pulling him apart in the market of Xianyang," the new capital he had built (Li 2013, 241).

Shang Yang governed for just twenty years, but his work set the stage for a strong and effective consolidation of power in China for generations afterward. Yin Yang, the first true emperor of China, built on the strengths of the Qin dynasty and his own skill in pulling military forces together. The dynasty firmed up the Great Wall and built an impressive road system of more than 4,000 miles.

To solidify his rule, Yin Yang created a system of civil administration, with 900 counties providing the empire's building blocks. The central government both appointed and paid each county's top officials. The officials, in turn, could not involve themselves in matters to which they were not appointed. When they were transferred to other positions, they could not bring their assistants along with them. The positions of these officials depended on their role, and the rules prevented them from building small empires of their own.

The government expanded Shang Yang's system of weights and measures throughout the empire. That was important not only for commerce but also for regularizing the government's power, since standard measures led to standard policies for taxes and standard pay for armies on the frontier. The Qin dynasty spread uniform currency throughout the empire, along with a standard system of writing. That put China far ahead of the French, where the Académie Française in 1635 was the first European council to bring uniform standards for language.

The Qin dynasty established a hierarchy, with power arrayed from top officials to local governments. Then, to staff the hierarchy, the government moved past hereditary power to a system of merit, where officials were hired based on their skills and judged according to competitive exams. This system was perhaps the world's first true bureaucracy, and it established the basic principles – a single ruler, hierarchical structure, hiring by merit, and selection by exams. To succeed in the exams, and ultimately in the government, the bureaucrats needed education. That was a privilege of wealthy families, and so the system reinforced a system of power concentrated in the upper class.

The fundamentals of the Qin system created a truly remarkable arrangement that became a model for governments over the next 2,500 years. The French philosopher Voltaire studied the Chinese system carefully in framing his own approach to the Enlightenment. He kept a portrait of Confucius in his office and praised his work, writing, "What more beautiful rule of conduct has ever been given since him in the whole world?" (Voltaire 1764, 238).

The basic rule of conduct might have struck Voltaire as beautiful, but its methods were anything but. The principles were elegant, but to institute them the Qin centralized power, burned books except for those it found useful, and imposed enormous taxes. The Qin dynasty left behind the rule of law that

Voltaire admired and the standardization of the Chinese language, as well as the Great Wall of China as well as the famed Terracotta Army of 8,000 life-sized warriors. But it also generated warfare on Yin Yang's death as competing forces fought for control of the country. The dynasty's effort to consolidate its control crumbled under the revolt generated by its iron rule.

It took the Han dynasty, which came to power soon afterward, to cement the cultural breakthroughs that the Qin dynasty launched. Its first emperor, Liu Bang, pushed the Qin forces aside and laid the foundation for the evolution of Chinese society. Years later, one of his successors, Wudi, not only expanded the dynasty's power but also established Confucianism as the state religion of China and created, in 124 BCE, an imperial university for educating bureaucrats, in what was likely the world's first school of public policy. This was not only important for reinforcing the power of the state. Wisdom was one of the fundamental tenets of the Confucian tradition, and that tradition in turn laid the foundation for centuries of Chinese reverence for facts and science (Provis 2019; Yang 2016).

There are even deeper differences that focus squarely on governance. Confucius argued that confidence in the state depended on the people's confidence in their ruler. That principle, in turn, proved powerful in shaping the Chinese government, far ahead of other governments, for millennia. To bolster that confidence and build the competence that the government needed, the government invented the merit system, accompanied by a civil service exam that gradually matured between 750 and 1250 CE. Especially in the earlier period, the Chinese civil service exam focused primarily on Confucian writing and interpretation, with increasingly more challenging exams for higher-level positions. Corruption was rare. Cheating, including bribing an exam grader, brought the death penalty (Peng 2018, 9–10). The system elevated a class of scholar-public officials who had a privileged place in the imperial court (Elman 2009). They worked extremely hard, but they also enjoyed great rewards.

The Chinese civil service system broke down class barriers even as it created them. Any talented young man could take the exam and, if successful, fulfill the Chinese goal of bringing honor to one's ancestors. The path to higher-level positions, based on merit, was open to everyone. And once candidates secured a place in the Chinese meritocracy, they enjoyed a privileged place in Chinese society. Individuals sat for three separate degrees: "Budding Genius," "Promoted Man," and "Achieved Scholar." The underlying foundation of equality of the system was remarkable, based on the classic writing:

> Human nature is basically good;
> Men are born approximately the same-
> Education makes the difference. (Han 1946, 160).

It was, Kellaway (2013) said, the "examination system from hell," which required memorizing 400,000 characters of Confucian text. The pass rate was just 1–2 percent. The "eight-legged essay" was a classic element of the exam, which required test-takers to create answers according to a fixed series of steps (legs). This construction ensured uniformity in the examination and grading process but, as the Chinese government approached modern times, critics also suggested that it created rigidity that in turn hobbled the country's development.

That has carried over within China to the present. Education has a high status in China, and teachers in China enjoy more respect in China than anywhere else in the world (Coughlan 2013; Leung 2018). These principles supported the development of public administration in China, support for the administrative system, the administrative system's support for the state, and the state's power, all for more than 2,100 years. Experts, power, and the state are inextricably linked.

Except for the influence of Confucian philosophy, China's ancient strategy for governance has been a rich lode for modern historians to mine. China's insights into the function of experts, the strategies for developing and controlling expertise, and the role of these traditions in governance play a powerful role in charting the ageless importance of experts in government.

Along the way, as Fukuyama (2011) has demonstrated, the issues of capacity and control became interconnected and inseparable. He contends that "successful liberal democracy requires both a state that is strong, unified, and able to enforce laws on its own territory, and a society that is strong and cohesive and able to impose accountability on the state. It is the balance between a strong state and a strong society that makes democracy work" (479). Creating a state with sufficient capacity to govern while not so strong as to abuse individuals is the central challenge for modern government, and it is the fundamental problem of public administration.

Even at the height of the Roman Empire, China was larger in size. Moreover, as Creel (1964) points out, "Far more than the Roman Empire, and more than any comparable state before modern times, it was administered by a centralized bureaucratic government" (155). It was, Creel contended, a system with "remarkable resemblances to the type of centralized bureaucratic government that is considered peculiarly modern" (157). "Its structure was formed," he concludes, "more than two thousand years ago, on the basis of an administrative philosophy that emphasized impartiality and impersonality," although personal relationships have often become "almost a religion" (183). This has always created real tension in China's governance. At the core, however, is the prominence of experts in Chinese governance.

In most countries, trust is highest in local governments and lowest for the national government. In China, it is precisely the reverse, in what analysts call "hierarchical trust" (Wu and Wilkes 2018). It is notoriously difficult to measure trust in Chinese governments, but Cunningham, Saich, and Turiel (2020, 3) found that satisfaction in the national government (93.1 percent) was higher than for provincial governments (81.7 percent), counties (73.9 percent), and townships (70.2 percent). Some of this pattern flows from the modern authoritarian nature of the Chinese government, but there are also deep roots that flow from the expert-based Confucian culture.

There is a long tradition that ascribes virtue to the emperor and that argues the need for a strong national government to protect people from the abuse of unscrupulous court officials and rogue local officials (Wu and Wilkes, 2018, 441). The culture has long put great emphasis on harmony, which in turn vested the experts in authority with great status (Zhou 2021).

The Han dynasty consolidated power in China and, over its 200-year rule, shaped a Chinese culture that long endured. In time, however, the dynasty collapsed. Not all its rulers proved equal to the challenge of governing a very large empire. Boy rulers became dominated by eunuchs, who numbered in the thousands and gained power through their access and loyalty to the emperor. Moreover, the government found itself squeezed between revenue shortages and peasants who resisted higher taxes in a series of rebellions. An ambitious general, Dong Zhou, tried to seize control by installing an eight-year-old puppet emperor, Xian, on the throne. But Dong's own bodyguard killed him in 191 CE, in an echo of Caligula's assassination on Rome's Palatine Hill 150 years earlier. Xian was forced from power, the dynasty collapsed, and competing warlords split up the kingdom.

The story of the Chinese roots of bureaucracy is one of the steady development of government expertise through a professional class and the institution of unifying threads, like language and culture. But it is also a story of the challenges of controlling the power that the ruling class created. Maintaining that system was expensive, and taxpayers resisted the government's hands in their pockets. The concentration of such power inevitably led to jealousy from competing forces, assassinations, and outright conflict.

Expert power once created proved hard to control. The Chinese did indeed invent the foundations of modern bureaucracy. But they also demonstrated the deep and inescapable tensions at its core.

The Roman Rule of Law

Along a very different path, the Romans developed a rule of law to advance governmental power. From its roads to the travels of armies who marched along them, Rome's rule marked a vast application not only of public programs but also of a system of governance, a system that lasted until the German push undermined the government in 476 CE, marking the decline and fall of the Roman Empire (Gibbon 1952). It is easy to forget that Roman history after the Caesars was nearly three times longer than the Caesarian era that the historian Suetonius (2007) popularized. That is a far longer period than any constitutional system since. The basic system of central power and a sophisticated system of administrative control emanating from Rome established the basic pattern of expertise that Westerners tend to see as the foundation for their governments, despite the long period of the Middle Ages, until the fifteenth-century Renaissance.

Rome is a testimony to bureaucratic expertise. Its buildings were remarkable not only for their style but also for their longevity. It is possible today to walk through the Roman Forum, still nestled between two of Rome's famous seven hills, and admire the triumphal arch, the house that kept the Vestal Virgins safe, the Curia where the Roman Senate met, and the temple where Julius Caesar was cremated. Much of the Colosseum remains standing, despite the damage caused by earthquakes in the fifth century CE. Recent renovations have opened the vast complex below the Colosseum's floor, where gladiators, animals, and their victims were kept before being escorted to the shows above.

Meanwhile, the Roman invention of a special kind of concrete – with "lime clasts" embedded in it – has helped some of the most striking pieces of Roman architecture, like the Forum, endure far longer than many far more modern pieces of construction. All roads indeed did lead to Rome, as Chaucer observed (1391, 2004) and some of these roads, including the Appian Way, remain in remarkable condition. The Romans needed the roads to quickly move armies to the far ends of the empire. Several aqueducts, designed to carry drinking water and constructed over nearly half a millennium, are still working. The famed Trevi Fountain in Rome is still supplied by an aqueduct built In 19 BCE.

The aqueducts were remarkable feats of engineering. Many are still standing, and that has allowed archaeologists to study their construction. The aqueducts relied on gravity, with a carefully measured slope designed to bring water from hills to where people needed water, all with measuring instruments that took engineers more than 1,000 years to improve upon (Matthews 1970). In southern France, for example, a Roman aqueduct is still in use, with its construction carefully designed to transport water for more than thirty miles, to Nîmes, with a drop of just fifty-six feet (Water Science School 2018). And to hold it all together, from the Colosseum to the Forum, the Romans invented their own brand of concrete and cement (Hunt 2023).

Roman rule grew on the expertise of its government officials. The Romans were famous for their military, from their fighting ships to the legions projecting power around the empire. They developed sophisticated supply chains to keep the legions fed and armed. The engineers responsible for the Roman roads, aqueducts, and other marvels typically came from the military. Trial and error produced daggers, swords, shields, bows, arrows, and other equipment that became carefully honed and standardized. Hospitals provided care to the wounded, and the soldiers could count on good food to eat – and beer to drink.

Meanwhile, the Romans developed a sophisticated approach to law, including law devoted to advancing the interests of the state and a separate body of law to deal with disputes between individuals. The influence of the Roman rule of law maintains a strong foothold in legal practice, including the use of Latin to establish basic principles, from habeas corpus to amicus curiae. Rome's expertise, from law to engineering, played a powerful role in establishing the remarkable breadth of its power and its centuries-long impact throughout the empire, through the civil servants who both invented and advanced this expertise. Roman laws had a tremendous impact on governments and their laws for more than 1,000 years.

Together, the world's great early governments established some basic truths. The ambitions of rulers to stabilize and expand their rule depended on power. That power came through bureaucracy and a special form of bureaucracy, the military. But it also worked in reverse. The bureaucracy and military, once established, became an independent power, whether it was Caligula's Praetorian Guard or China's ambitious Dong Zhou. To prevent that power from undermining their own rule and ruffling the people, especially in the taxes they had to pay to support bureaucratic power, leaders established a rule of law – guardrails to shape the exercise of power and to keep it in check. A leader's power depended on gathering the expertise ne'ded to rule. That expertise became institutionalized in bureaucracies, shaped by the rule of law. But the bureaucracy, once established, can easily drift into an independent power source, one without which a ruler cannot rule but one that, at the same time, can prove hard to control.

There can be no government without power. There can be no government power without bureaucracy. And there can be no bureaucratic power that does not contain within it the implicit challenge to a ruler's rule.

The Greek Foundation for Experts

However, that leads to the fundamental question about just *who* should rule, especially in a democracy. There's a fundamental dilemma. Should the people rule? Or should experts make the decisions? Would rule by the people lead to responsive but ineffective policies? Or would rule by experts improve the chances for good results but produce an unaccountable government?

These issues preoccupied Plato, who explored these puzzles in detail, especially in his most famous work, *The Republic*. His masterpiece, written about 380 BCE, did not tackle the puzzle directly. Instead, he created a long series of dialogues featuring his mentor, Socrates. Plato has Socrates explain that "the State" – government – "is not one but many, like a bazaar at which you can buy anything" (Book VIII), from making big policy to doing nothing, from waging war to choosing peace.

If that is democracy's great virtue, it also creates nothing but problems, because pure democracy pays no attention to the education of experts. He has Socrates explain, "Observe, too, how grandly Democracy sets her foot upon all our fine theories of education, – how little she cares for the training of her statesmen! The only qualification which she demands is the profession of patriotism. Such is democracy; – a pleasing, lawless, various sort of government, distributing equality to equals and unequals alike" (Book VII). In fact, he worries, "does not tyranny spring from democracy" (Book VIII). Plato contends that the ideal state that he has in mind "may really come into being when there shall arise philosopher-kings, one or more, who will despise earthly vanities, and will be the servants of justice only" (Book VII). These philosopher-kings acquire the education and training not only to understand the best way to solve problems at hand but also to bring a sense of ethics, to ensure that the government's actions are the best actions. The solution to the fundamental puzzle, Plato has Socrates explain, is that "the perfect guardian must be a philosopher." Indeed, "until philosophers bear rule, States and individuals will have no rest from evil" (Book VI).

For the next 2,400 years, humankind has debated the approach that Plato laid out – and has constantly searched for such philosophers. If governance in the hands of non-experts is lawless and rudderless, does governance by experts risk an expert-based oligarchy that brings its own pathologies? Plato worried that democratic rule cannot resolve the ethical dilemmas facing the state. With the rule of experts comes the accumulation of power. And, as Caligula discovered some 400 years later, concentrated power can create a deep state that can be impossible to control. It can also become a power dangerous to rulers who falsely think they might control it. That created the foundation for exploring what the ideal rule of law might look like, and what role knowledge ought to play.

That puzzle inevitably found itself entangled with the growth of bureaucracy, which became the essential building block for modern society and the source of inevitable scorn. As Otto von Bismarck quipped, "The bureaucracy is what we all suffer from." But we often suffer as well from the failure of bureaucracy without the expertise needed to solve the problems that we want solved.

4 Knowledge

For centuries, the Roman Empire was by far the most powerful force on the globe, both in the expansion of its provinces and in the impact of its laws. But in the fourth century CE, Rome's hold on those provinces began to disintegrate as Goths swarmed into some of the provinces as they fled the Huns. Rome's army began to collapse amid civil wars and the rising power of barbarian tribes. Much of what was left of Roman imperial rule moved east to form the Byzantine Empire, but with far less clout than Rome had enjoyed at the height of the empire's power.

It fell to the Byzantine emperor Justinian to try to restore the empire's former glory. He managed to pull Italy, Sicily, and Rome itself back into the empire's rule. But perhaps most important, he sponsored the rewriting of Roman law. Justinian's code provided the bridge to the Enlightenment and built the foundation of legal authority in Europe as it emerged from the Middle Ages and, indeed, to the legal framework in many countries today. The effort required truly extraordinary knowledge.

The foundation for distributing this code, along with other fruits of Roman thought, came with a remarkable invention. Through at least the time of the Caesars and perhaps through the third or fourth century CE (historians are not sure), scribes produced the written word on strips of papyrus, which were then rolled onto long scrolls. The Romans began replacing the scrolls with the codex, a remarkable innovation (Hartmann 2020). Parchment replaced papyrus because it proved smoother and more durable. That made it possible for scribes to write on both sides. Parchment could be bound, usually on the left, and put between covers, which provided better protection. Pages could be numbered and volumes could be indexed. These books still had to be written by hand – that would not change until Gutenberg invented the printing press in the mid-fifteenth century, which made possible the first mass distribution of a Bible and a Psalter – but the invention of the codex allowed the Romans to broadly distribute the knowledge they were generating. Nothing was more important to this base of knowledge than the rule of law.

Formalizing the Roman Rule of Law

From his base in Constantinople, Justinian aimed to bring the Roman Empire together again. From his base in the east, he stitched together parts of the old territory. And he set to work recapturing the remarkable collection of Roman laws and legal opinions from the Empire's earliest days. The effort began with significant linguistic challenges, since Greek was the prime language of the East and much of the Roman legal tradition was in Latin. Leading Justinian's effort was Tribonian, a Greek who had established himself as a major legal Byzantine legal figure.

Legal proceedings had become complex and lengthy because of the vast collection of laws and precedents, so Justinian concluded that the laws needed to be consolidated. Tribonian's team pulled together previous legal collections, reviewed all of them, tossed out the ones they decided were no longer relevant, and sorted them into a consistent framework, with clear subjects. Some laws conflicted with each other, so they decided which ought to rule. In other cases, they clarified what the law actually said, to root out misinterpretations that had crept in over time. By 529 CE, Tribonian and his team completed the first part of the code, with three more parts following in subsequent years – 1,000,000 words in all. Law professors assembled the state of legal knowledge into fifty books, making the changes they thought were necessary. Justinian promulgated their work as *Corpus Juris Civilis* (translated as the body of civil law). And he also distributed a legal textbook, called the *Institutiones,* for use by beginning law students (McSweeney and Spike 2015, 21).

By the sixth century, the government had become more ambitious. Law had become the center of government. Legal scholars studied and codified the law. And law students devoted themselves to the knowledge of governance. There were laws covering every stage of life, from marriages to commerce to criminal penalties. (The compilation is available today in an electronic version, in the original Latin version, composed of six volumes [1606].) Justinian thus institutionalized Roman law. His efforts to reclaim Rome's past glory through conquest dissolved, but the *Corpus Juris Civilis* had lasting impact.

In the west, however, the force of the *Corpus* evaporated along with Justinian's reconquests. For 500 years, until the eleventh century, Justinian's masterwork was mostly unknown and, by most accounts, lost to scholars. The loss was what made the Dark Ages especially dark.

Rediscovering the Lost Rule of Law

This did not mean that there was no rule of law to shape the West in these centuries. The enduring threads came from the Catholic Church and its *jus canonicum,* or canon law. When the Roman Empire and the *Corpus Juris Civilis* faded away, the church and its legal structure remained, along with ecclesiastical laws to shape the institution. As John C. Wei and Anders Winroth (2022) point out,

> Before the modern era, it had as much influence on the daily life of Europeans as secular law has on life in the modern world. It touched nearly every aspect of medieval society, dealing not only with what most people today would

consider to be religious matters but also with many issues of a purely secular nature. Trying to understand medieval Europe without knowing medieval canon law is like trying to understand the Renaissance without ever having read the Bible or the Latin and Greek classics: impossible yet not uncommon.

That became even more important with the rediscovery of Justinian's *Corpus* in northern Italy during the eleventh century. No one knows exactly why it disappeared, although it is likely that it faded away with the Roman Empire in the west. And no one knows quite how it reappeared. With the *Corpus,* though, medieval monks were able to reconnect Roman civil law with the church's canon law.

Leading that effort was a monk named Gratian, who took up the job of pulling together all the existing canons of the church into *Concordia Discordantium Canonum,* or simply the *Decretum,* in much the same way that Justinian led the effort to consolidate Roman law. It was a job of enormous complexity because, just as had been the case for Justinian, the canons of the church's law had grown over time into many contradictions and problems. Meanwhile, in the absence of Justinian's code, civil law was confusing and, often, not very civil at all, with trial by ordeal replacing the rule of law that the Romans had built over time.

Gratian's major accomplishment was remaking the elements of canon law into legal coherence and then integrating it with Justinian's *Corpus.* At that point, there was no separation of church and state. The church provided the ongoing expertise that carried the rule of law forward. Learned monks maintained maintaining writing and reasoning, and they translated it for civil authorities (Baldi 2010).

The links between these two bodies of law were important for the church as well after the schism between the Roman and Eastern Orthodox churches that erupted in 1054. The Eastern church grew on Greek philosophy, while the Roman church remained rooted in Roman law with its heavy Justinian flavor. Gratian did for the church's canon law what Tribonian had done for Roman law. He further integrated canon and civil law into a system that shaped governments in the Middle Ages. He brought a bright light to illuminate the Dark Ages, and his work became the textbook of learning.

The work of Gratian and his monastic brothers reinforced the institutionalization of knowledge that marked the Middle Ages. If Justinian helped spread the study of law through the creation of legal textbooks, the church's monks professionalized the study of law. Their work fostered the creation of institutions devoted to the study of law, and the institutions in turn led to the foundation of some of the world's great universities. Coming first in the Roman tradition was the University of Bologna in 1088 (although Morocco's University of Al Quaraouiyine was founded in 895 and remains the world's oldest university).

As McSweeney and Spike (2015) noted, "the rise of Roman law is inextricably bound with the rise of Europe's first university, the University of Bologna." In fact, "People would travel from all over Europe to study with its legal luminaries, who established rock-star-like reputations that spanned the continent" (22). Students then took Bologna's lessons back to their home countries, where the important blend of civil and canon law shaped governance throughout Europe. That reinforced the legitimacy of Europe's rulers, since they were grounded in high learning. It also established the legal standards by which they would be held accountable (24).

From this foundation, bureaucracies sprouted to study, advance, and apply law. The law that they promoted, moreover, was a merger of civil and canon law. In fact, there was a Medieval proverb that stated, "A Romanist without canon law isn't worth much and a canonist without Roman law is worth nothing at all" (McSweeney and Spike 2015, 25). It became impossible to count oneself among the educated if one had not mastered the combination of the work of Gratian and Tribonian, and the combined force of Roman civil law and the church's canon law.

Other universities followed the Bolognese model, with the creation of the universities of Paris (1045), Oxford (1096), and Cambridge (1209), as well as others throughout Europe. Divine provenance did not hurt their efforts – the belief that God inspired the church and that the church's laws were the manifestation of that inspiration. That reinforced its power in shaping modern legal doctrine (Foley 2009). The Roman Catholic church is the oldest continuously operating legal system in the Western world, although the Chinese system we saw previously continued to operate in the East with its own rule of law. In the Muslim world, Tunisia's Ez-Zitouna University is also the oldest continuously operating university in the world. Religion, learning, and expertise have always been closely linked.

The Bridge to the Enlightenment

The religious foundation of the rule of law in the Medieval Age was important in several respects. Before the rediscovery of *Corpus Juris Civilis,* the Catholic Church's canon law provided a legal structure for governance. In many courts, religious and civil law was indistinguishable, both because of the significant power of the church and because embracing the religious power provided added legitimacy for civil rulers. After the *Corpus* reappeared, both civil and canon law remained intertwined, now with the added force of the consolidated doctrine.

That power endured for centuries, especially because Gratian's codification of canon law established the study of law as distinct from theology. That, in turn, established the foundation for the civil law that guided kings and emperors through the late Middle Ages. Meanwhile, Gratian's consolidation of canon law provided the foundation for the church's legal structure until 1917, when the Catholic Church revised its canon law.

Without the role of the church, the Dark Ages would have been even darker. The church provided the essential bridge from the destruction of Roman rule in the West during the late fifth century to the Renaissance of the fifteenth and sixteenth centuries. The church was rich enough and powerful enough to sponsor some of the great works of the Renaissance, like Michelangelo's *Pieta* and the construction of St. Peter's Basilica in Rome. It was not an easy time for the church, especially in the early Renaissance when three men simultaneously laid claim to being the pope and when the Protestant Reformation got its start. But by this point, civil powers had generated enough power and standing to act independently of the Catholic Church, although many rulers remained staunchly religious, and even less religious kings found legitimacy in their religious roots.

All this grew out of the role of experts, especially religious monks, who maintained the fundamentals of society – reading and writing – and established its foundations – beliefs supported by law. They did not rule, but without them, rule would have been far different, without the legal structure that pushed aside trial-by-combat and duels. These experts were the bridge to modern society, especially during the Enlightenment in the eighteenth century (Lehner 2015).

Many elements of the Enlightenment, in fact, threatened the church and its hold on expertise. Johan Gutenberg's printing press democratized knowledge by making it easier for people to acquire things to read. It was far easier to print large quantities of books than for monks to painstakingly copy a codex by hand. The printing press, in turn, made it possible for Martin Luther to spread his critique of the Roman church. Natural philosophers like Galileo shook the church's hold on science by demonstrating that the earth was not the center of the universe, and Isaac Newton framed fresh ideas about basic scientific, non-religious theories about human existence.

When it comes to the role of experts in government, Enlightenment thinkers laid out a very different philosophy, not governed by the church but rooted in the rule of law. The chain of ideas began with Thomas Hobbes, who famously argued that the state of nature was unruly, with life that was "nasty, brutish, and short." How should people work within such a state of nature? They needed a government to establish and maintain order.

This government would have great power to deal with the pessimistic world state of the world that Hobbes described. John Locke and Jean-Jacques Rousseau took a more benign view of the state of nature, where people are free and equal but where they risk using their freedom in ways that harm others. To ensure such protection, the government must be powerful. To control that government, they create a social contract, in which people surrender some of their rights to the government in exchange for the government's protection of their rights and property. If the protection disappears or if the king becomes a tyrant, the people have the right to throw off the government's power and establish a newer, better one. That, of course, provided the foundation for Thomas Jefferson's Declaration of Independence and the grand American experiment in governance.

Property was an essential element of these philosophers. Locke, for example, wrote about the need to protect "life, liberty, and property," which Jefferson later changed to "life, liberty, and the pursuit of happiness." This was not a rhetorical flourish, because Locke saw a direct link between happiness and property (Macpherson 1962; Nozick 1974; Ryan 1965; Simmons 1992; Tuckness 2020; Tully 1980).

This philosophical argument, in turn, laid the foundation for Adam Smith's *The Wealth of Nations* (1776). His highly influential treatise argued that theories focusing on agriculture and trade were too limited. Instead, he contended that free-market competition would produce the most efficient use of a society's scarce resources. That competition, in turn, would produce an equilibrium, which would on the whole leave everyone better off.

Smith marked the transition from an institutional to an individual view of expertise. The church and its rule of law would no longer have sway over the structure of society. Some of his biggest fans have held him up as a God-fearing, religious-leaning, tireless advocate of unfettered capitalism. All these characterizations are either wrong or, at the least, subject to debate among scholars. Some scholars like Jacob Viner (1927) held that held that Smith was religious at his core. Others, like Ronald Coase (1976), contested that view, contending that there was scant evidence that "to which Adam Smith was committed to a belief personal God." Instead, Smith wrote of the importance of "Nature" or "the great Director of Nature" or even, most famously, "the invisible hand" (538).

This debate is important for two reasons. One is the question of the motivation for Smith's "invisible hand." It is possible to debate just how strong a force his belief in God was in advancing this notion. But more important, for our purpose here, is to note that it was that markets relied on individual actions. The other is that, with the rise of these individual motivations, the institutional role of the church in shaping society receded. With Hobbes, Locke, Rousseau, and Smith, the previous dominance of the church and its canon law receded. That framed Smith's views about the role of government in shaping the exercise of these individual motivations. Many of Smith's fans hold him up as the central figure in arguing for unfettered market capitalism, with the government taking a hands-off approach. However, as economist Herbert Stein (1994) points out, that's anything but the case.

Stein's wonderfully entertaining essay contends that many of Smith's fans "wear the Adam Smith necktie as a sign that they are CPC – Conservatively Politically Correct." The goal is "to make a statement of their devotion to the idea of free markets and limited government." But Smith, Stein contended, "did not wear the Adam Smith necktie." Moreover, "Smith was prepared to look at the conditions of his time and make a judgment, reflecting a presumption against government intervention, about whether government action in particular cases was appropriate. His admirers do not have to accept his judgments. But they should accept the idea that such judgments have to be made." Smith certainly believed in the benefits of market competition and the freedom to buy and sell to produce an efficient allocation of goods and services. But he also contended that such competition risked benefiting the rich at the expense of the poor. He recognized, as Stein pointed out, that government had a role in setting the guardrails of competition and dealing with its more damaging implications.

So, with the rise of Enlightenment thinkers, the importance of experts in government had grown as the central role of the church faded. It remained useful to invoke the Almighty. The British sovereign remained head of the Church of England, and Catholic rulers occupied key thrones in Europe. In the United States, of course, there was far more tension around the issue. The nation's founders insisted on a separation of church and state but, at the same time, most of the country's first universities grew up with religious ties.

The core issue, as Stein points out, was just how many governmental fetters there ought to be on capitalism – and what responsibility government ought to take on in addressing the problems that free-market competition generated. These tradeoffs, of course, are at their core political questions. But their answers inevitably require governmental capacity: experts who know how to marshal the government's power to solve the problems and to stay out of the way when free-market competition beckons.

The rise of individual rights thus marked an important transition away from more than 1,300 years of an ecclesiastically driven rule of law. It marked a shift in the role of experts, to support a new kind of institutional role supporting democratic governance. And it raised a new puzzle: how to institutionalize and control this new breed of experts.

5 Institutions

By the 1700s, private markets were fueling global trade, especially in Asian spices. This created the first real debates about the tensions between public and private power – and between expert and popular control of government.

The result was the re-emergence of the civil service, along Chinese lines but under a more-Romanesque rule of law. It was a system designed to balance private expertise and democratic power.

The Rise of the British Civil Service

Exotic spices had been in great demand for 4,000 years, both to provide unique fragrances to homes and to add novel flavorings to food. Europeans especially relied on trade with warmer regions, since wonderfully fragrant and tasty spices like cinnamon, turmeric, and ginger did not grow well in the chilly climates. It became impossible to think of the British without tea, and the British could not obtain their tea without trade.

In the East, people had savored tea for thousands of years. The British aristocracy caught on to the habit but, because it was so expensive, they treated it as a treasure. As trade expanded, however, tea became one of the great social levelers, although the savory, milder tea remained the drink of the rich while the working class drank strong, black tea, which required milk to make it more palatable. In time, everyone enjoyed their tea with milk, with the royal family pouring their tea first and adding their milk afterward (Barrie 2018). Over the years, however, whether to pour the milk before adding the tea or tea before adding the water became a class issue in England before disappearing in all but lore by the 1970s (Markmanellis 2017).

It is impossible to exaggerate the hold that tea has acquired on British society, where people drink 100 million cups of tea each day, or 36 billion cups per year (UK Tea and Infusions Association 2023). It did not hurt that far more Britons carry a genetic variant that allows them to digest milk as adults, compared with their European neighbors (Ashworth 2021), but that of course created further distance between the Britons and non-tea-drinking neighbors.

In the late fourteenth century, struggles over the spice trade provoked a war between Genoa and Venice. Venice won, but other countries sensed the growing value of spices and struggled to break into the business. In fact, one of the main goals of Christopher Columbus's exploratory voyages was to help Spain find a shorter route for trade and, in the process, break Venice's stranglehold on the spice routes. For Spain, new naval passages seemed especially promising for finding a piece of the business, which had become the new frontier for global competition.

The Dutch, meanwhile, created their East India Trading Company in 1602, following on the heels of the English East India Trading Company, founded in 1600. The defeat of Spain's armada in 1588 gave the English an opportunity to disrupt the existing monopolies, and the expansion of English trade in India and

China helped cement the nation's economic – and political – empire. Tea, of course, is not native to England, and the growing tea-drinking culture of England demanded a steady supply. The demand for the beverage, along with the vast array of other spices and products from the East, vastly increased the English East Trading Company's influence.

Its economic power brought the company political power as well. It not only became an economic behemoth. Its expanding reach brought it control of Bengal and that, in turn, gave the company and its shareholders enormous political power over trade policy. Since influence at shareholder meetings could be wielded by those who bought up the company's shares, the potential for corruption grew, which prompted William Pitt the Younger to lead a parliamentary effort in 1784 to regulate the company's power. They eventually ended the company's economic monopoly, and by the mid-1800s it became an agent for the British Raj.

As the company's role grew, its officials concluded that they needed to train employees for the roles they were playing. That led to the establishment of a training academy in 1796, to create a professional cadre of corporate officials to head the company's work. As the company's economic ties became inter-woven with its political power, its work also became more entwined with the government in London.

That, in turn, made its work part of the "civil" structure of the country – "civil" meaning it pertained to citizens, derived from the same Latin root – and it did not take long for this effort to give birth to the phrase "civil servant." The company's growing power and reach created increasing demands for access to jobs, even for individuals who had not graduated from the traditional training grounds of Oxford and Cambridge (Civil Service History, n.d.; Coolican 2018; Lowe 2011). And, given the company's reach and power, its influence on the British government was enormous.

That fueled a debate about how best to build on the British tradition of governance through experts while, at the same time, allowing elected officials to exercise control. At the time, because of the connection between private and public power, the British government was plagued by favoritism through corruption. There was growing concern that experts with the best ways of managing government problems were sidetracked by paternalism and venality. As Martin Stanley (n.d.), a former senior civil servant and historian of the British civil service, pointed out, "Rulers have always needed civil servants – and especially tax collectors." Moreover, "They also needed filing clerks." For example, despite all his considerable faults, King John worked very hard to create a good recordkeeping system following his signature on the Magna Carta. These records, in turn, "were effectively the means used by royal government to get stuff done."

How should the British government deal with the growing challenges of regulating the economic behemoth? A plan emerged from a report, written by Stafford H. Northcote, who later was appointed as chancellor of the exchequer, and C. E. Trevelyan, who was the Treasury's permanent secretary. Northcote and Trevelyan (1854) argued that the government's civil service ought to radically shift its focus from its existing closed system of hiring, which relied heavily on the Oxbridge pipeline, to one based on competition through exams and appointment based on merit. They contended that

> the Government of the country could not be carried on without the aid of an efficient body of permanent officers, occupying a position duly subordinate to that of the Ministers who are directly responsible to the Crown and to Parliament, yet possessing sufficient independence, character, ability, and experience to be able to advise, assist, and to some extent, influence, those who are from time to time set over them. (2)

The existing system was by no means attracting the best and brightest, they said. Instead, "admission into the Civil Service is indeed eagerly sought after, but it is for the unambitious, and the indolent or incapable, that it is chiefly desired" (4). They were heavily influenced by the Chinese Imperial Examinations, which led them to recommend "the establishment of a proper system of examination before appointment, which should be followed ... by a short period of probation" (9). And what subjects ought to form the basis of the examination? The focus, they concluded, should be on "history, jurisprudence, political economy, modern languages, political and physical geography, and other matters, besides the staples of classics and mathematics" (14).

The Northcote–Trevelyan report was broad and path-breaking. It took several decades for the recommendations to work their way into the fabric of the long traditions of the British government, but the report created the modern foundation for experts in democracies: open access to the civil service, instead of recruitment from a closed circle of those with deep connections; selection of employees based on their merit, instead of through favoritism; identification of merit on the basis of standardized exams, instead of through arbitrary criteria; career service, with promotions based on performance; and responsibility to political executives and the parliament for the exercise of their power, instead of creating independent and unaccountable power centers.

Their report laid out the basic principles for both creating and controlling experts in the British government. It established the core that led to the development of the British civil service over the following centuries. A British guide for new civil servants, written just after World War II, explained it like this:

Oddly enough there is no simple and authoritative definition of the term "civil servant." The word "civil" is easy enough; "His Majesty's civil establishments are those of His Majesty's establishments which are not military, i.e. not part of the armed forces. "Servant" needs a little more thought.

Legally, you serve the King. That means, in practice, that you serve the responsible Minister in charge of your Department, who exercises powers as a member of His Majesty's Government; and since the Minister is responsible to Parliament, you serve Parliament, and hence the community. . . .

As a civil servant, you must never forget that, however well qualified and expert you may become in your job, you have not been elected to it by any vote; and in a democratic country is the elected representatives – Parliament – who must settle the lines on which the government of the community is to work. In other words, as a civil servant you are not entitled to do things according to your personal taste just because it is your personal taste. You must do what Parliament wants you to do. . . .

Your loyalty is to the Minister of the day. When a new party comes into power, your new Minister may require radical changes in the policy of your Department. Your duty is to carry out the new policy with the same loyalty that you gave to the old. (HM Treasury 1949, 5)

These core ideas, of both principle and process, guided the creation of the modern British government, and they spilled over into the American civil service system a few decades later.

The Birth of the American Civil Service System

The first decades of the American government saw a gradual shift to partisan preference in hiring government officials. When the presidency shifted for the first time from Federalists to Democratic-Republicans, in the transition from John Adams to Thomas Jefferson, Jefferson felt obliged to "redress the balance" among government employees. This meant appointing "only Democratic-Republicans until a balance between his party and the Federalist Party was attained" But, in general, the first six presidents "were able to develop a civil service which, while not perfect, was of high quality. The civil servants of that day had both ability and integrity. It was a good civil service for its time," reported the government's official and definitive history of the civil service system (US Office of Personnel Management 2003, 11, 15).

But the Jackson administration made big changes that endured for decades:

It became routine for the incoming President, his Cabinet, and the heads of agencies to put aside all other business for the month following the inauguration, in order to concentrate on settling the aggressive and conflicting claims of the hordes of officeseekers who descended like locusts on Washington. The struggle for jobs caused much bitterness, and jobs were openly bought and sold. . . . The result of this type of patronage [for clerical positions\ was to

load the Federal payroll with persons who were hired not for their ability to do
a job but because of their inability to find a job elsewhere. (16–17)

In the Jackson administration, the claims of office seekers grew fierce. Mobs
elbowed their way into the White House after his inauguration, demanding jobs
and cleaning out the snacks provided to guests. Jackson believed in both
patronage and in the value of periodic house cleaning so that job holders
would not develop a sense of proprietary rights to their positions. Political
claims and even payoffs for positions were commonplace. Job seekers even
placed newspaper ads offering kickbacks for an appointment. By the time of
Martin Van Buren's inauguration, Washington bristled with 40,000 people
seeking jobs, some even setting up camp in the White House (21–22).

In the 1870s, Ulysses S. Grant's proposals for reform by hiring federal
government employees based on merit faltered when Congress cut their
funding. Some champions of reform, however, continued the campaign,
with none more important than Sen. George H. Pendleton (D-Oh.).
Pendleton had a rich pedigree, as the son-in-law of Francis Scott Key, who
wrote the "Star Spangled Banner" and who was the Democrats' vice-
presidential nominee in the unsuccessful effort to unseat Abraham Lincoln
in 1864. Pendleton's initial efforts bore no fruit, however. The existing spoils
system had too many friends, among those who received federal jobs and
those empowered to give them out. But that all changed following the assassination of President James A. Garfield in 1881.

That crime emerged from the sordid underbelly of American politics. At the
time, many politicians believed that government appointments were "gifts
given at the pleasure of powerful officials to those who had been most useful
to them," as historian Candice Millard put it in her story of Garfield's death.
That was certainly what his killer, Charles Guiteau, believed. Just four months
into the president's term, as Garfield entered Washington's Baltimore and
Potomac Railroad Station (now the home of the National Gallery of Art),
Guiteau fired two shots at the president.

Garfield was seriously wounded, but he seemed on the verge of recovery until
an infection, due in part to his wounds and in part to the clumsy efforts of
multiple doctors to remove a bullet, took his life on September 19. Millard noted
that, with the months of suffering that Garfield endured, "it became clear that the
nation had changed not just suddenly but fundamentally and irretrievably"
(Millard 2011, 202). In the opinion of just about everyone, Guiteau was
delusional, having convinced himself that he was responsible for Garfield's
victory because of that a single campaign speech, which one writer has called
"incomprehensible." In exchange for what he believed was his invaluable

support, he roamed official Washington to press officials in the new administration for a position he was convinced he deserved. His top choice was in Paris, in the diplomatic service.

Guiteau had made a pest of himself in the White House and State Department. In one encounter, an exasperated secretary of state James Blaine told Guiteau, "Never bother me again about the Paris consulship as long as you live." Guiteau convinced himself that Blaine and Guiteau both posed a danger to the republic and that the only way to solve the problem was to kill the president. In his later written confessions, he wrote, "His removal is an act of God." Guiteau said, "In the president's madness, he has wrecked the once Grand Old Republican Party; and for this, he dies" (*Report of the Proceedings* 1882, 1486). Guiteau's violent retribution for what he believed was Garfield's slight was notable for its insanity. With his gun, as one writer put it, he became "the most hated man in America" (Resnick 2015).

His expectations for a federal job, however, were nothing out of the ordinary. In fact, they had been part of the very fiber of American politics since the days of President Andrew Jackson. After Jackson's victory, New York senator William L. Marcy (Dem.) declared "that to the victor belong the spoils," and the quote famously gave birth to the role of the "spoils system" in filling federal positions (White House 2020). Jackson believed that the public service should be democratized and that its work could – and should – be done by ordinary people.

If ordinary people could do the job, then rewarding political allies with the jobs solved the problem of staffing the government and rewarding friends. In practice, Jackson neither embraced the spoils system as enthusiastically as his critics would later contend nor advanced the role of the common person in government as much as his rhetoric promised. But the basic notion – that government jobs ought to be given to political supporters – became entrenched in American politics.

The practice led to "periodic chaos" with every change in administration, as Frederick C. Mosher (1968, 63) put it. Claimants for federal jobs wandered Washington's streets and hallways, and presidents and their cabinet members found themselves constantly put upon by what Leonard D. White (1958, 6) called "the never-ending importunity for office," as knocks on the door came constantly with friends, new and old, looking for federal jobs.

Grover Cleveland's Interior Secretary Lucius Q. C. Lamar complained, "I eat my breakfast and dinner and supper always in the company of some two or three eager and hungry applicants for office; go to bed with their importunities in my ears" (White 1958, 6). The constant churn of positions created deeply rooted political machines designed to fill them. In turn, this produced a growing sense of government incompetence, and undermined public confidence in government.

The spoils system came to define the government corruption that, Americans became convinced, had led to Garfield's death and the American government's poor performance.

In his first address to Congress, Garfield's successor, Chester A. Arthur, made an impassioned case for civil service reform. His ideas, he said, were "in conformity with the existing civil-service system of Great Britain," the initiative that had grown from the Northcote–Trevelyan report, "and indeed the success which has attended that system in the country of its birth is the strongest argument which has been urged for its adoption here." America urgently needed a reform that took the best of the British system (and avoided some British innovations that had stirred objections in the United States, including life tenure for civil servants, exclusion of older individuals from applying for positions, and a retirement pension). The key elements of an American system, he told Congress, ought to embrace important values:

- *Competence*: "No man should be the incumbent of an office the duties of which he is for any cause unfit to perform."
- *Lessons from business:* "It seems to me that the rules which should be applied to the management of the public service may properly conform in the main to such as regulate the conduct of successful private business."
- *Testing*: "Original appointments should be based upon ascertained fitness."
- *Steadiness*: "The tenure of office should be stable."
- *Promotion based on merit:* "Positions of responsibility should, so far as practicable, be filled by the promotion of worthy and efficient officers."
- *Accountability*: "The investigation of all complaints and the punishment of all official misconduct should be prompt and thorough."

These views, Arthur (1881) concluded, "are doubtless shared by all intelligent and patriotic citizens, however divergent in their opinions as to the best methods of putting them into practical operation."

Arthur, a Republican, made common cause with Pendleton, a Democrat, to create a new merit-based system for the federal government. Arthur supported Pendleton's act in 1883 and, in his 1884 State of the Union address, the president celebrated the victory. "The system has fully answered the expectations of its friends," he told Congress, "in securing competent and faithful public servants and in protecting the appointing officers of the Government from the pressure of personal importunity and from the labor of examining the claims and pretensions of rival candidates for public employment" (Arthur 1884).

Debate had been brewing for years about reform, but it took Garfield's assassination to move it forward. As was the case for the British reform, the Pendleton Act initially covered just 10 percent of the federal government's workforce (Pendleton Act 1883). Like the British reform, it took many years for its procedures to settle into place. But its ideas set the stage both for reforms and debates that followed.

Moreover, in Arthur's comments, there was a stone that continued to rub in the shoes of the American civil service for generations. In his argument about the lessons from business, he advanced the idea that government ought to be run more like the private sector. The interconnection of public and private ideas about government employment was nothing new, of course. The British system, after all, had emerged from the work of the East India Company, and the work of government reform had been enmeshed in the government's connections with the big private company. The East India Company had been a huge success, so reformers assumed that they must have been doing something right. There was also an underlying assumption that the government was backward, needed to catch up quickly, and that private experience provided the best model.

The Fundamentals of the American Civil Service System

The Pendleton Act brought a fundamental revolution to governance in America. It was, Paul Van Riper (1958) wrote, "an orderly retreat of parties from their prerogatives of plunder" (105; see also Ingraham and Rosenbloom 1990). It asserted the importance of experts in government, based on three fundamental points that echoed the fundamentals of the Chinese civil service established millennia before:

- *Fair competition* for federal jobs, open to everyone.
- *Neutral competence,* based on politically impartial examinations.
- *Political protection,* ensuring that government civil servants were insulated from coercion and undue influence from elected officials and their political appointees.

The act focused mostly on the issue of the day: how best to hire based on merit instead of political favoritism. It did not deal with an issue that became heated a century later: how best to remove poor performers. Like everything else since the very beginning of civil service systems in China, its story is a tale of gradual evolution.

Strengthening the government's competence was essential to the act, but the model left unanswered the big question: How can elected officials keep the mastery of facts by civil servants be kept under political control? How can political officials prevent their civil servants from creating a "deep state"? Those were questions that deviled the evolution of the American civil service over the next generation.

6 Ripening

Toward the end of the nineteenth century, the size and span, and reach of government, in the United Kingdom and the United States and other rapidly industrializing nations, increased considerably. That, in turn, significantly grew the power of the bureaucracy and vastly fueled the challenge of keeping it under control. As Stephen Skowronek (1982) has chronicled, the modern administrative state began to emerge as a product of new challenges and deep traditions. The result, as Daniel P. Carpenter (2001) describes, was a trend toward bureaucratic power that grew into bureaucratic autonomy.

In the century after the passage of the Pendleton Act, the American civil service gradually grew into an ever larger and more powerful system. Officials were keenly aware that the competence they were building into the civil service also sharpened the fundamental question with which governments had been dealing since Roman times: How could government create the competence it needed while holding that power accountable?

Before he left academia for the presidency, Woodrow Wilson formulated an answer. In the early days of the American republic, he wrote, the challenge was to determine "how law should be administered with enlightenment, with equity, with speed, and without friction" (Wilson 1887, 197, 198, 201). As government became more complex, the job was to make the government's "business less unbusiness-like," while at the same time developing mechanisms of control. Wilson mused that "the English race" had "exercised itself much more in controlling than in energizing government." The public deserves good administration; a focus on popular sovereignty makes it hard to deliver.

How to solve this riddle? Wilson's answer was to drive a wedge between the *deciding* of government policy and the *doing* of it. It was possible, he concluded, to strengthen capacity without threatening control because "administration lies outside the proper sphere of *politics*." "Administrative questions are not political questions" (210). Administration, in turn, required discretion. "The cook must be trusted with a large discretion as to the management of the fires and the ovens," he wrote, ensuring that "meddlesome" public opinion did not interfere with administration (214, 216). The key, he concluded, was separating the cook's work from the policy decisions about the menu.

This formulation, which became known as the politics-administration dichotomy, framed the theoretical debate in American public administration for decades. The dichotomy, he believed, would allow the government to create robust administrative capacity without sacrificing political control. Wilson's position got support from luminaries like Frank J. Goodnow, who wrote one of the very first influential books in the field, *Politics and Administration* (Goodnow 1900). For many scholars in subsequent generations, however, Wilson's solution was a bit too neat. For some, its value "persists not as a guide to behavior but as an intellectual device connecting practice to theory" (Montjoy and Watson 1995, 231; see also Svara 1985; Waldo 1984). The core critique was that politics and administration were inextricably linked. And if they were interconnected, they could not practically be separated.

If Wilson's answer was unsatisfactory to many theorists, it at least had the virtue of neatly framing the question. It fell to the country's leaders in the twentieth century to frame an answer by expanding the coverage of the civil service system.

The Growth of the Civil Service

The Pendleton Act initially covered mostly employees in post offices and customs houses, where the buying and selling of jobs had been most common. Over time, however, the share of workers covered by the civil service system increased from 10 percent in 1883 to 41 percent in the McKinley administration. It grew to 41 percent in the McKinley administration, increased further through the Teddy Roosevelt and Wilson administrations, and hit 80 percent in the Hoover administration, as the government steadily grew.

The number dipped during the Franklin D. Roosevelt administration, first because the New Deal demanded a quick increase in federal employees and the administration did not want its signature program to hit delays. That same logic expanded even further during World War II, when the war effort required quick staffing increases to manage procurement, and administration officials worried that the civil service hiring process would slow down the war effort. By the end of the Truman administration, however, the postwar government modernization spurred the maturation of the civil service system and nearly 90 percent of all federal employees were covered by the civil service system (see Table 1).

But this did not mean that Franklin D. Roosevelt was unconcerned about how best to staff the government with experts. He appointed a three-member committee of public administration superstars – Charles Merriam, Luther Gulick, and chair Louis Brownlow – to take an exhaustive look at the federal government's needs. Their principal conclusion was that "The President needs help." To give the president the help needed, the committee laid out an extensive plan for reform of the federal establishment, especially the regulatory agencies that were emerging across the government (President's Committee on Administrative Management 1937, 5). Their recommendations outlined the framework for the modern executive branch, and their background papers provided a wealth of thoughtful and influential analyses (Gulick and Urwick 1937).

Table 1 Growth in the civil service

Year	Administration	Percent covered by the civil service system	Prominent issues
1883	Arthur	10	Began with passage of the Pendleton Act; initially included only Washington departments, post offices, customs houses
1901	McKinley	41	Expanded through executive order
1907	T. Roosevelt	64	For first time, merit system exceeded number of jobs in spoils system
1918	Wilson	70	Expanded as part of modernization
1932	Hoover	80	Expanded as part of further modernization
1936	F.D. Roosevelt	60	New agencies exempted from civil service as part of emergency start-up during New Deal
1938	F.D. Roosevelt	66	Incorporation of agencies into civil service
1945	Truman	33	Many positions created on "war service indefinite" basis – for duration of war, plus 6 months
1949	Truman	84	Ramping up of examination process; veterans preference rose from 16 percent to 47 percent
1952	Truman	86	Maturation of civil service system following the 1949 act

Source: US Office of Personnel Management (2003).

The Brownlow Committee recognized the central importance of ensuring the accountability of administrators to policymakers in Congress. "The preservation of the principle of the full accountability of the Executive to the Congress is an essential part of our republican system," the committee wrote. But for the committee, the more important line was between policy-determining positions at the very top of the bureaucracy, which "are relatively few in number," and the rest of the bureaucracy, which ought to be part of the career civil service. "An increase in the number of higher posts included in the civil service will lift its entire morale and will give an incentive for the recruitment of the best talent in the lower positions," the committee wrote (President's Committee on Administrative Management 1937, 43, 8). The committee argued passionately for greater competence in government, and its three commissioners concluded that the best way to draw the politics–administration line was between the career service and department secretaries and other political appointees. Its members saw accountability as a two-part effort: of top officials, to Congress for making policy decisions; and of the rest of the federal bureaucracy, to expertise for shaping policy results. The committee sought a substantial expansion of the civil service system, to "include all permanent positions in the Government service except a very small number of a high executive and policy forming character" (President's Committee on Administrative Management 1937, 7).

The report, however, attracted withering political attacks, especially because critics believed that the committee was proposing a transfer of legislative powers to the executive. That, of course, reflected the old arguments, dating from the country's founding, about how the president had the authority to dismiss political appointees like ambassadors. The Brownlow Committee's work got caught between conflicting views of public administration, a congressionally centered approach on one side and strengthening executive power on the other, as well as political clumsiness in making the case for the recommendations (Brownlow 1958; see also Roberts 1996). Even though the committee's recommendations failed on Capitol Hill, over time "the new administrative order that the committee championed is ascendant, and the committee's goals for regulation have been achieved in principle," Perri Arnold wrote (2007, 1030–40). On the report's basic strategy for strengthening the executive branch, there was surprisingly little pushback. Indeed, as Mosher (1968, 82) points out, "The Brownlow Committee itself seemed little troubled by the politics–administration dichotomy."

The 1949 Classification Act

The twin governance crises of the Great Depression and World War II pushed thoughts of civil service reform to the sidelines. The Roosevelt administration worried about responding quickly to each of these challenges in turn. It developed new agencies whose employees were not covered by the system and, as a result, the share of federal employees covered by the civil service dropped by more than half, from the pre-war high-water mark of 80 percent to the postwar low of 33 percent. The war dramatically expanded the size of the US government, with many ad hoc organizations invented on the fly. When the war ended, Truman asked former president Herbert Hoover to chair a commission charged with examining the government's operations from top to bottom. In personnel, the administration won passage in 1949 of the Classification Act, which marked a substantial expansion of the civil service's size and structure (Leich 1953).

The act marked the most fundamental legislation since the enactment of the Pendleton Act two-thirds of a century earlier. Among other things, it established a simplified "general schedule" of salaries, with each position in the government assigned a salary grade. This general schedule set pay by position, not by the person filling that position, and each agency gained the authority to classify its own positions. It expanded the number of positions covered by the civil service and created the basic structure of the civil service that has endured since. Hiring was competitive, based on a merit-based examination designed to test the employee's qualifications for a position. Each position was classified at one of the eighteen grades in the general schedule, and the grade determined the person's salary. Individuals could move within their grade up through a series of steps, primarily through longevity, and each step increase brought a higher salary. Promotions were based on merit.

That focused the work of the government's civil service managers on classification: taking each of the federal government's career positions, identifying the skills needed, and assigning each position to a place in the general schedule. Over time, Congress could increase wages, but everyone's salary increase depended on their place in the schedule, not on their individual characteristics. The basic goal was to separate federal employment from the influence of politics. But by concentrating on the relatively mundane and arcane questions of classification, it also tended to push the civil service system to the sidelines of American politics and its debates about the big questions of what government programs the country ought to pursue.

Ripening Tensions

It did not take long for the neat system imagined by the 1949 act to become unraveled. In 1952, Dwight D. Eisenhower became the first Republican president in twenty years. The new administration naturally came to the White House concerned about whether the many new civil servants, hired during the Democratic years, would be responsive to the new administration. It was a challenge, Mosher (1968, 85) noted, of "how to make a public service, in theory largely civil service protected and politically neutral, responsive to new political leadership." Complicating the issue were the relatively small number of political

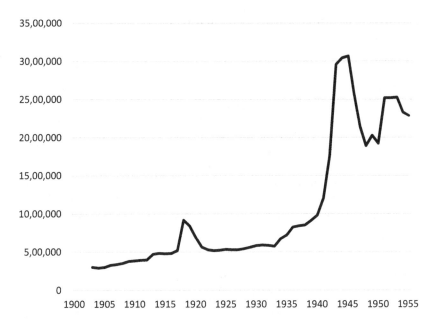

Figure 1 Federal executive branch employment

Source: 1939–1955 – Federal Reserve Bank of St. Louis. (undated). "All Employees, Federal," *Federal Reserve Economic Data,* https://fred.stlouisfed.org/series/ CES9091000001; and for earlier years, US Bureau of the Census. (1949). *Historical Statistics of the United States, 1789–1945.* Washington: US Dept. of Commerce, Table P 62–68, 294,

appointments that Eisenhower had at his disposal, the relatively few Republicans who had substantial federal experience, and the attack on government employees waged by Sen. Joseph McCarthy's witch hunt for communists.

Even after the war effort wound down, the federal establishment was vastly larger than in the pre-war years, as Figure 1 shows. The federal workforce more than quadrupled from 1933 to 1953. It was one thing to argue for a professionalized civil service under one party's control. But it was quite another for the workforce to reckon with the transition to a different political party in the White House.

To ensure he had experts he could count on in key positions (Lewis 2010), Eisenhower created a new "Schedule C" in the federal service, which followed Schedule A (to increase the representation of individuals with disabilities and to permit the hiring of experts whose qualifications are impossible to examine, like physicians, attorneys, and chaplains) and Schedule B (for positions where competitive examinations are difficult to conduct). Schedule C allowed him to place far more political appointees in key positions throughout the government. Over time, that also vastly increased the reach of politics into administration. He also appointed a new study commission, headed again by Hoover. In its second volume, the commission laid out the basic problem:

> In the 160-odd years since a two major-party political system developed in the United States, the American people have sought to achieve a workable balance between two vital requirements in the management of their Federal civilian employees. One requirement ... is that the officials responsible for establishing and defending Government policies and programs, the noncareer executives, should be selected by the successful party. ... The other requirement is that there must be numerous trained, skilled and nonpartisan employees in the Federal service to provide continuity in the administration of the Government's activities. (Quoted in Citizens Committee for the Hoover Report 1955, 3)

Like the Brownlow Committee report, the Hoover Commission's second report had little immediate impact on the operation of the federal government. But it sharply framed the central question: ensuring the government's expertise while keeping it responsive to elected officials and, ultimately, to the people.

In the years following World War II, academics became increasingly wary of the artificial division between politics and administration. For Paul H. Appleby (1949), public administration was fundamentally a political process. Norton E. Long (1954) argued that the quest for a value-free, expertise-driven was a waste:

> However attractive an administration receiving its values from political policy-makers may be, it has one fatal flaw. It does not accord with the facts of administrative life. Nor is it likely to. In fact, it is highly dubious even as an ideal. Though the quest for science, mathematical precision and certainty has an undeniable psychological appeal, it runs the risk of becoming a fastidious piece of ivory-tower escapism. (22)

After all, the 1950s was a time when science was triumphing on every front, from the development of mainframe computers to the mastery of the hydrogen bomb – every front, that is, except in government, where the deep paradox between control and capacity emerged.

Government programs had never been more complicated or more in need of experts to manage them. New political officials, however, were deeply suspicious that the experts they found on taking office would resist new policies. What point, after all, was there in winning an election if the government could not be harnessed to advance the policies of the winners? But what good would there be in advancing those policies if the bureaucracy did not have the expertise to administer them well?

Bureaucracy and the "Good Life"

Since Plato and Aristotle, humans have struggled with this issue. How societies resolve it defines the very nature of the way they define how they view "the good life," as Dwight Waldo (1948) put it in *The Administrative State*, a classic work of public administration framed in political theory. Those involved in both the management of government as well as the study of public administration, no matter how technically focused they claim to be, certainly have their own visions of what that "good life" ought to be, who ought to advance it, and how they ought to do so.

Waldo believed that the Good Life must be planned and that the planning must grow out of a sense of the public interest. In his view, the introduction to the Brownlow Committee's report defined the basic puzzle:

> Our goal is the constant raising of the level of happiness and dignity of human life, the steady sharing of the gains of our Nation, whether material or spiritual, among those who make the Nation what it is. ... By democracy we mean getting things done that we, the American people, want done in the general interest. Without results we know that democracy means nothing and ceases to be alive in the minds and hearts of men.

At the core, the challenge was how best to marshal administrative capacity without sacrificing democratic control. At the core of the battle was the role of the expert administrators who work within the government.

Civil servants found themselves caught in the crossfire between opposing camps. One camp was the case for growing the government's capacity because the increasing complication of the government also required increasing expertise to manage it. The other was, ironically, an increasing politicization of the civil service, where government employees became the center of a growing proxy war: bureaucracy transformed from its role as an instrument of policy to a symbol, as well, of the government's size and power.

Government bureaucracy has long been a symbol of the government's power. After all, Roman legions marched forward with a standard at their head, emblazoned with "SPQR," short for *Senatus Populusque Romanus,* or the "Senate and the People of Rome," because the state wanted to remind both those who saw the standard and those who fought for it what the stakes were. (The acronym is so deeply ingrained in Italian society that, in the first part of the twentieth century, the fascist government inscribed it on utility covers and fountains throughout Rome. Many of the inscriptions remain today.)

Ratcheting Up Political Responsiveness

If administrators have always been a symbol of the political issues swirling around government, they have increasingly also become the focus of attacks on the "deep state." Some critics have paradoxically viewed the bureaucracy as independently powerful, while others have contended that administrative red tape render the bureaucracy not powerful enough.

The tension between these positions deepened at the end of the 1960s. This remarkable and turbulent decade had seen a dramatic celebration of the role of experts, such as the rocket scientists who answered President John F. Kennedy's 1962 call to put a man on the moon by the end of the decade, which NASA accomplished in July 1969. Kennedy appointed Robert McNamara to lead his Defense Department, and he in turn brought in "whiz kids" from the RAND Corporation to transform the Pentagon's analysis, operations, computing, and management practices.

By the end of the Johnson years, analysts struggled to understand why the administration's War on Poverty seemed to produce disappointing results. The Republican presidential candidate Richard M. Nixon's campaign slogan, "Bring Us Together," pledged an end to the civil strife that had erupted in the late 1960s. He harnessed that to his "law and order" campaign to win key votes in the South. When he won the presidency, Nixon surprised everyone with genuinely ambitious efforts to devolve power from Washington to the state and local governments. As the foundation at his presidential library later recalled, "If there was a single animating principle behind Nixon's good-government reform efforts, it was this: *lessen the power of the federal bureaucracy*" (Nixon Today 2017).

It was not an anti-expert, anti-bureaucracy position. Rather, it was an anti-federal-bureaucracy view. For example, he surprised Democrats with a plan to devolve decision making over federal aid to state and local governments through General Revenue Sharing, which distributed money automatically by formula, to every general-purpose state and local government in the country, and through block grants, which converted many traditional federal grant programs into clusters that gave state and local governments far more discretion over how to use the money. In a stroke, he pivoted away from the federal government's accumulation of power, which was at the core of Johnson's "Great Society" programs, and the role of federal administrators, who exercised strong control over who got how much money for which programs.

Nixon, however, did not stop there. He waged a clandestine war against his enemies, with firm pressure inside the administration to use the federal government's vast resources for revenge against the president's enemies.

Top administration officials identified "who they feel we should be giving a hard time," as a memorandum entitled "Dealing with our Political Enemies" put it. The goal, said the president's counsel, John Dean, was "how we can use the available federal machinery to screw our political enemies." The plan envisioned a "project coordinator" who would take the enemies list, and "then determine what sorts of dealings these individuals have with the federal government and how we can best screw them (e.g., grant availability, federal contracts, litigation, prosecution, etc.)" (Dean 1971).

Nixon's approach to the bureaucracy, as with everything else during his presidency, was buried in a deep paradox. He launched programs that grew out of generations of Republican ideology focused on shrinking the size and power of the bureaucracy, especially the federal bureaucracy. But on a level not previously seen in the modern era, he sought to use the bureaucracy's power to reward friends and punish enemies. The former had its roots in principle. The latter grew out of his effort to gain control. The bureaucracy was, at once, a source of frustration and power: frustration at a bureaucracy he believed was blocking his agenda and power to employ that bureaucracy to advance his political goals.

Throughout the evolution of bureaucracy from ancient times, we have seen each of these instincts. Not until the Nixon administration, however, did we see such a simultaneous, aggressive effort to embrace both sides of this paradox.

Carter's Modernization of the Civil Service

In the aftermath of the Nixon administration's scandals, the Carter administration in 1978 championed a major civil service reform to push aside the political abuses of the Nixon administration while enhancing the civil service's expertise and political responsiveness. There was broad consensus in Washington that a new president had a right to expect the bureaucracy would use its power to pursue the president's program. There was also a consensus that this bureaucracy needed skilled managers who could tackle the challenges of the late twentieth century – and that a resolution of these issues ought to be fitted within the rule of law. Carter sought to rebalance the political equation.

The 1978 act flipped the previous century's growth of the civil service on its head. Rather than separating the civil service from politics, it aimed to make the civil service more responsive to the president's policies and leadership. As OPM's official history of the civil service put it, "while the public holds the President, as Chief Executive, accountable for everything that happens during an administration, the President had no effective means of exercising executive control over the massive civil service" (US Office of Personnel Management 2003, 148).

As Carter noted in a memorandum to agency managers following the law's passage, the 1978 law was revolutionary. Among other things, it:

- "Creates a Senior Executive Service as a government-wide corps of more than 8,000 top executives to manage Federal programs of all types.
- Bases the compensation of Senior Executives and GS13-15 managers on individual and organizational performance.
- Provides the statutory framework for new systems of performance appraisal within the agencies as a basis for advancement and retention of employees.
- Gives managers throughout government more flexibility and authority in all phases of personnel management so they can hire, motivate, reward, and discipline employees as necessary to carry out their programs.
- Provides employees with fairer protection of their legitimate rights, including protection against political abuse." (Carter 1978)

The combination of a new tier of top executives, performance appraisal linked to performance pay, flexibility in hiring and discipline, and broader protection of employees' rights (through a new Merit Systems Protection Board) was, by any measure, the most forward-looking human capital policy in the nation's history. In fact, it marked the high-water mark of confidence in the ability of an expert government to be responsive and a responsive government to be expert.

It did not take long, however, for the law's ambitions to become sclerotic. In fact, a generation later, there was a single overriding consensus: almost no one, Republican or Democrat, much liked the civil service system – even the modernized system that Carter had championed.

7 Sclerosis

Since the 1980s, the system became ever more focused on process and far less on mission. That distorted the role of the civil service within the government and fed the ongoing hardening of the procedures that, in turn, undermined the tradition of bipartisan support for the civil service that had developed over a century.

The sclerosis of the system grew out of reinforcing instincts. Stakeholders, especially public employee unions and veterans' groups, pushed hard to reinforce the rules that advantaged them. Democrats argued for more government employees and a stronger role for public employee unions. Republicans, on the other hand, saw the civil service as an engine that grew the government's size and enhanced the Democrats' power. Just about everyone complained that it was hard to fire poor performers. As one former official explained, it *was* possible to fire a civil servant, but the effort could take months and occupy an inordinate amount of time. "A manager might go through that process and win," the official said, "but only do it once." The process was simply too painful (interview with the author, 2023). Ed Everett, a former city manager, along with co-author Mary Welch, contested the conventional wisdom, however. Firing poor performers was in fact possible, he argued. "There are tons of excuses, but never good reasons for not dealing with poor performers" (Everett and Welch 2023).

From ancient times, the purpose of government experts in the bureaucracy was to advance the government's mission. The debate has for millennia swirled around how best to achieve that mission, what that mission was, and how it might shift with different rulers. Issues that might seem mundane issues of management are, in fact, the most fundamental issues of politics. The colliding storm fronts in the decades after the passage of the 1978 act made the system a lightning rod for the rising political battles about what government ought to do and how big it ought to be.

In the Eisenhower years, Paul Van Riper wrote an extensive study of the development of the American civil service (1958). He noted the long period of political support that had grown up around the system and how the makeup of the civil service mirrored society far better than in other major democracies. But he also concluded that the system had become top-heavy, with too much centralization, too little flexibility for operating agencies to meet their missions, and too many rules that hamstrung the system. His analysis foretold the controversies that were to cripple the system over the next two generations.

The civil service system had few friends. It generated legions of enemies, on all parts of the political spectrum, committed to trimming its size, scope, power, and process. The bipartisan consensus that had supported the system since 1883 was beginning to crumble. President Ronald Reagan led the early counterattack. He came to the job determined to cut as much of the bureaucracy as he could. Instead of Nixon's more subtle effort to devolve bureaucratic authority, Reagan wanted to eliminate it. And instead of marshaling the bureaucracy's power to serve political ends, Reagan wanted to shrink it. Bill Clinton came at the challenge from the perspective of his "reinventing government" strategy, designed to "create a government that works better and costs less." The system emerged from the ongoing battles with few friends.

Sclerosis of Ideology

Ronald Reagan's administration marked a fundamental break from previous approaches by both Democrats and Republicans to the challenge of building experts in government. Rather than pursuing the strategy that presidents of both parties had advanced – strengthening and expanding the number of experts inside government – Reagan sought to shrink the federal workforce through privatization and outsource many of the experts it needed. The privatization movement was a fundamental shift in the notion of what experts the government required and where it could get the expertise it needed.

The preceding centuries marked a gradual effort to build competence through experts, control through a rule of law, and institutions to set the balance. Conservative thinkers, however, advanced the argument that government administrators sought to increase their power by increasing their budgets (Dunleavy 1985; Niskanen 1971). This growing power, therefore, made them harder to control.

Reagan famously quipped, "The nine most terrifying words in the English language are: I'm from the Government, and I'm here to help" (Reagan 1986). The same year, Terry Cullen, a former senior OPM official in the Reagan administration, wrote an acerbic *Wall Street Journal* op-ed, contending that the government "should be content to hire competent people, not the best and most talented people, in a deliberate play on David Halberstam's famous title, *The Best and the Brightest* (1972). "A good case can be made," Cullen argued, that the "best and the brightest" employees "are needed in the private sector where wealth is produced rather than consumed" (Cullen 1986).

How could governments deal with what conservatives claimed was the fundamental instinct of government experts to increase their power? Conservative economists of the rational-choice school had two answers. First, since they believed that the pressures toward budgetary expansion were hardwired into the behavior of government experts, the only way to deal with them was to have fewer experts. Governments could be more efficient by cutting the number of administrators. Second, since there were important responsibilities that the government needed to perform, the government could rely on the self-correcting forces in private markets, where market competition produced greater efficiency than government monopolies. That led to the argument for privatization: eliminating as many government functions as possible and, for the functions that remained, turning service delivery over to private companies.

The first step in Reagan's playbook was the launch of his own commission, headed by private sector executive J. Peter Grace. The commission's report concluded that government could find $10.5 trillion in savings, especially from privatizing many government functions (Grace Commission 1984). Within a few years, the initiative led to the contracting out of tasks ranging from cafeteria services to aircraft maintenance were contracted out. But there was a supreme irony in the administration's efforts. Although it did indeed privatize many services, the administration had to hire many new federal employees to manage the defense buildup which was also a major administration priority. By the end of the Reagan administration, there were actually more federal employees than at its beginning.

Despite the mixed success of the Reagan initiatives, the privatization strategy marked a dividing line between the long development of the career bureaucracy, on the one hand, and the rise of an ideological view of bureaucrats, on the other. Conservatives began viewing experts as a heavy weight on the federal budget and a sluggish impediment to its work. The conservative solution was to eliminate as many of them as possible. On the other hand, liberals saw the effort to eliminate federal workers as an assault on federal programs and on the administrators themselves. Conservatives, they believed, had found they could not cut many programs with which they disagreed, so they focused instead on weakening the government's ability to carry them out. The civil service often became less an instrument of government action than a symbol of the developing basic ideological battles of the last quarter of the twentieth century.

Even the Clinton administration found itself caught in these struggles. As part of its "reinventing government" movement, it cut 426,000 federal workers (Kamarck 2013). The cuts added to reinventing the government's credibility; they provided the "costs less" side to the "works better, costs less" formula. In making the cuts, however, there was little attention to just how many employees the government needed to do its work. The revinenters were caught in the ongoing debate.

The cuts significantly reduced the number of federal employees, but the upward drift in the number of federal employees 'soon resumed. During the George W. Bush administration, there was a form of reverse privatization: the government responded to the September 11 terrorist attacks by bringing airport screeners, who had worked primarily for private companies, into the federal government. It also established the new Department of Homeland Security, which further fueled the need for federal workers. The basic ideological struggle over the role of government experts, however, had become fixed. Reagan marked the high-water mark of the Republican effort to shrink the role of government experts, through his policy of privatizing as much federal work as possible. On the other hand, Carter marked the high-water mark of the Democratic effort to enhance the role of a politically impartial cadre of government experts.

Against this backdrop, the composition of the federal workforce changed dramatically. The number of federal civilian employees in 2023 was actually smaller than fifty-five years earlier, at the close of the Johnson administration. However, Reagan's privatization movement had dramatically reduced the number of blue-collar workers, who had done everything from clean federal buildings to

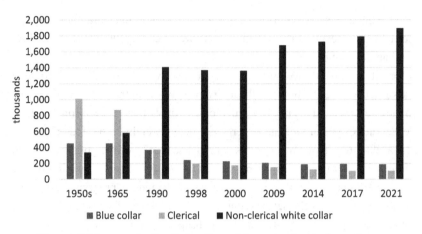

Figure 2 Changes in the federal workforce by type of employee

Source: Jeff Neal, https://chiefhro.com/2014/09/18/do-we-need-a-million-fewer-fed eral-employees/comment-page-1/; and US Office of Personnel Management, FedScope.

guarding their entrances. The number of clerical employees shrank as well, as automation transformed the nature of work. But the number of non-clerical, white-collar federal employees more than quintupled from the 1950s to 2021 (Figure 2). These were the experts inside the federal government, and they were the experts needed to run the expanded array of government contracts. Reagan's strategy to pare the size of the federal government was important ideologically. In practice, however, the pace of growing the federal government's expert class was dramatic.

Sclerosis of Process

It did not take long after the 1978 Civil Service Reform Act, moreover, for the system to become trapped yet again in its old problems – the "excessive rules, slowness, and apparent lack of accountability and sensitivity to the world beyond bureaucratic boundaries," as Patricia W. Ingraham (2006, 487) wrote. The system's basic principle might have been merit but, as Ingraham noted, "civil service systems are not meritorious in many ways (468)." Instead, she wrote, there were "dysfunctional bureaucratic characteristics of the civil service system" (487). The sclerotic forces clogged hiring, in particular. It became one of the biggest manifestations of what Jonathan Rauch (1995) called "demo-sclerosis: the silent killer of American government."

Bureausclerosis in Hiring

Agencies were often nervous about spreading their wings under the Civil Service Reform Act. The Office of Personnel Management (OPM) was created to manage the act's provisions, but the agency soon became trapped in the deep ideological tensions surrounding the civil service. In fact, OPM never had the chance to find its footing because, soon after the act's passage, the Reagan administration's privatization strategy sought to sideline it. During the Clinton administration, the downsizing initiative operated independently of OPM's planning.

The combination of these political tensions with the challenges of administering the complicated Civil Service Reform Act tied the personnel system up in regulatory knots. In 2001, for example, a fifteen-year federal manager complained, "I can assure you, from my experience, that federal employees are extremely protected from dismissal, and this leads to all kinds of games." If supervisors believed that it was hard to get some employees out, potential employees complained that it was hard to get in. "I have tried for three years to get a government job, to no avail," one prospective employee complained to the *Washington Post*. "I have a master's degree. . . . I have applied for numerous positions . . . even stated I was willing to relocate. Nothing!"

On the hiring side, a federal employee noted that the hiring process was "byzantine" because of "personnel who do not understand or comprehend the rapid changes in job requirements" but who had to approve job announcements. As a result, "the time it takes to finally offer a position is so long that many applicants already have taken other jobs" (Barr 2001). These were constant complaints about the federal personnel system, from both applicants and hiring managers, and they continued for decades. The actual time-to-hire for federal employees was 106 days in 2017, inching up from 87 days in 2012. In comparison, the typical time in the private sector was 23 days, in 2014 (Katz 2018).

The comparison of public and private hiring left OPM with few friends. Federal agencies with political clout won separate, flexible hiring authorities outside OPM's realm. By 2016, GAO counted a staggering number of these authorities – at least 105 in 2016. Even though the hiring authorities proliferated, federal agencies used just a small number of them, with just 20 authorities used in hiring 91 percent of their new employees (US Government Accountability Office 2016). "As a result," a study by the National Academy of Public Administration concluded, "the federal civil service system has become a non-system: agencies that have been able to break free from the constraints of the outmoded regulations and procedures have done so, with the indulgence of their congressional committees." (National Academy of Public Administration 2017, 3). Agencies without political clout found themselves handcuffed to rules that other agencies has escaped.

More flexibility led to less coherence – a case of what the National Academy of Public Administration called "an advanced case of *bureausclerosis*, caused by increasing administrative layers and walls between policymakers and the administrators charged with carrying out policy" (11). Moreover,

> government occupations and the nature of much government work have changed radically, but the government's human capital system has barely changed at all. The result is like trying to negotiate the high-speed internet with only an old electric typewriter (12).

As a result, the system collapsed into a focus on rules because that proved far easier to navigate than a focus on the mission. Of course, managing the rules often provided little connection to managing the mission.

Sclerosis from Special Preferences

Complicating the problem of federal hiring was the creation of veterans' preference, where many (but not all) former members of the armed forces got a bonus number of points in the hiring process.

Preference in the hiring of military veterans dates to the Revolutionary War, when former officers (but not enlisted soldiers) received a preference in hiring for federal jobs. Legislation formalized the preference during the Civil War and expanded it to honorably discharged members of the military. In 1944, Congress established the modern version of veterans' preference. In support of the bill, President Franklin D. Roosevelt wrote, "I believe that the Federal Government, functioning in its capacity as an employer, should take the lead in assuring those who are in the armed forces that when they return special consideration will be given to them in their efforts to obtain employment" (US Office of Personnel Management, n.d.).

This preference was important in recognizing veterans for their service to the country, but it also disrupted hiring for merit in the federal government. Thirty percent of all federal employees are veterans, and almost 90 percent of those veterans were hired through veterans' preference. Disabled veterans, who receive an extra preference, accounted for 46 percent of all veterans in the federal workforce (Interagency Veterans Advisory Council 2021). Out of all new hires in the federal government in 2020, 25 percent were veterans, and 22 percent of new hires had veterans' preference (US Office of Personnel Management 2022, 13–14), while the number of veterans in the overall popula-tion was 6 percent. Out of all federal employees, 30 percent are veterans, and almost 90 percent of those veterans were hired through veterans' preference. Disabled veterans, who receive an extra preference, accounted for 46 percent of all veterans in the federal workforce (Interagency Veterans Advisory Council 2021). On one hand, veterans gained an extra advantage in federal hiring. On the other hand, non-veterans often found themselves locked out of many federal jobs, since the bonus system pushed most vets ahead of them in the hiring queue.

Veterans' preference thus created a fast track around the basic merit system rules. But the process did not always work well for veterans over the long term. Turnover for veterans hired by the federal government proved significantly higher than for non-veterans. Within their first five years, veterans left the federal workforce at nearly a 70 percent higher rate. Veterans were less satisfied than non-veterans with their relationships with their supervisors and with the meaningfulness of their work (US Government Accountability Office 2020a).

Veterans unquestionably deserve a privileged place in the application process because of their service to the nation. But the system of veterans' preference that gradually emerged over time vastly complicated the hiring process, undermined the focus on merit, made it difficult for non-veterans to get government jobs, and did not always serve the veterans themselves well.

Sclerosis from Unions

Union representation of the US workforce has gradually been declining, dropping from 20.1 percent in 1983 to 10.1 percent in 2022. In the private sector, unions represented just 6 percent of private-sector employees, compared with 33 percent of government workers (US Bureau of Labor Statistics 2023). Unions increasingly depended on organizing government employees to retain their political strength.

Some of the conservative attacks on unions focused on their organizing power, funded by union dues. Wisconsin Republicans, for example, restricted dues collection by public unions, in retaliation for the unions' support of Democrats. In weakening the unions, Republicans transformed the balance of political power in the state from blue to purple or leaning-red (Kettl 2015).

More fundamentally, conservatives contended that unions prevented managers from managing. As Philip K. Howard (2023) writes in *Not Accountable,* "Accountability is basically nonexistent in American government" because "performance doesn't matter." The reason, he said, is that "police unions, teachers unions, and other public sector unions have built a fortress against supervisory decisions." As a result, "the operating machinery of government grinds along at half capacity or less" (8–9).

The rising power of unions, in turn, led to the shrinking leverage of elected officials over elected officials. This independent base of power, Howard (2023) contended, made unions in particular, and the civil service in general, unconstitutional. He wrote that "several specific provisions of the Constitution explicitly safeguard against the delegation of sovereign powers (128)." However, "Public union bargaining and political activity have supplanted or materially weakened sovereign power" (129). "America's constitutional republic is not structured to accommodate an outside power independent of the will of the people." Therefore, "The disempowerment of elected public employee unions has undermined this basic premise of constitutional government," Howard concluded (133).

Sclerosis of Politics

Many of these issues, of course, flowed from the inherent tension baked into the civil service system: developing expertise to accomplish the government's mission while also promoting loyalty to the regime in power – a balance that Hugh Heclo (1999, 132) called "loyalty that argues back." That, of course, is the basic principle behind the Westminster system of government, with its emphasis on advice to the "government of the day." Over time, however, the focus on expertise made it hard to achieve loyalty, or at least political responsiveness. The system's conservative critics contended that the problem began with the power of public employee unions and extended to what they said was the fundamental unconstitutionality of the civil service system itself (Howard 2023).

To complicate matters, the ongoing battles over the role of the public service undermined the role of the federal government's central personnel agency, the Office of Personnel Management. It became caught in the crossfire between those seeking to strengthen the basic steering role for the human capital system; battling to protect the power of the public employee unions; and campaigning to shrink the number of government employees. As a result, the rudder for steering government-wide human capital policy steadily became disconnected.

Sclerosis: Trump's Counter-attack

Howard's argument grew from the aggressive effort during the Trump administration to remove protections from many federal employees. At the very end of the administration, the president signed an executive order creating a new "Schedule F" that gave him the power to fire officials at will who had "a confidential, policy-determining, policy-making, or policy-advocating character" (Executive Order 13957, October 21, 2020). Schedule F was a new part of the civil service regulations, following Schedules A through E, which already gave the president the power to appoint a significant number of officials. With its broad language, Schedule F covered a vast number of officials, potentially in the hundreds of thousands of federal employees.

While working for the Trump administration, James Sherk led the campaign. He contended, "Career employees should give their best advice to political appointees, but once politically accountable officials make a decision, career staff should implement it faithfully." Instead, "Career employees routinely delayed producing new rules or produced drafts that couldn't be used," "frequently withheld vital information from political appointees," and "often wouldn't work on cases they opposed for ideological reasons." He concluded, "This behavior undermines our democracy. No one votes for career bureaucrats, and they have no authority to replace elected officials' policies with their own" (Sherk 2022b).

Liberals and, especially, public employee unions fiercely pushed back. They claimed that the effort was illegal and totally inconsistent with the merit principles of the civil service. Most constitutional lawyers, however, concluded that the president's power to issue the executive order was in fact legal. More fundamentally, critics argued that it was profoundly unwise (Wagner 2020).

Trump's electoral loss in the 2020 presidential election made the issue moot, at least for the time being. Soon after taking office, Joe Biden issued his own executive order revoking Schedule F (Executive Order 14003, January 22, 2021). But Biden's order scarcely ended the debate. For the conservatives behind Schedule F, the Trump effort was part of a long-run strategy to shrink the size of the federal government, to make it easier to fire federal employees and to break the back of what they viewed as the "deep state" crippling their policy efforts. It was nothing less than a strategy to change the balance between capacity and control, by putting the accountability for all federal officials at center stage and pushing away from a focus on capacity.

The conservative case against the "deep state" built on arguments about past debates and current performance. As Sherk explained (2023),

> You need accountability in the government. If we are going to have government by consent of the governed, then the government needs to answer to the people's elected officials. And right now there are major impediments to that, particularly with these civil service protections. I think that to realize the democratic ideals that this nation was founded on, the bureaucracy needs to be fully accountable, and that includes the bureaucracy. . . . One aspect of it is the ability to fire every federal employee, who should serve at the pleasure of the president. Then he is accountable to the American people for how he manages the overarching enterprise.

Sherk contended that the founders intended for the president to have broad removal power over members of the executive branch. In the debate over the Constitution, James Madison (1789) said:

> If the president should possess alone the power of removal from office, those who are employed in the execution of the law will be in their proper situation, and the chain of dependence be preserved; the lowest officers, the middle grade, and the highest, will depend, as they ought, on the president, and the

president on the community. The chain of dependence therefore terminates in
the supreme body, namely, in the people; who will possess besides, in aid of
their original power, the decisive engine of impeachment.

In writing the Pendleton Act in 1883, which created the foundation for the civil
service system, Congress did not include protections against the dismissal of
poor performers. The extensive protections of civil servants grew up over time,
especially since World War II. So if the country looks back to the lessons of the
founders, both of the Constitution and of the Pendleton Act, there is the
presumption that the president can remove poor performers because Article II
of the Constitution imposes on the president the duty to "take Care that the Laws
be faithfully executed." That was the foundation for Schedule F and for the
broader argument that the president has the power to insist on accountability of
all government employees – and to remove those who do not perform well.

History does not support this line of argument. Although Madison did indeed
make that argument about the "chain of dependence," he was talking about
individuals with presidential appointments. In writing about others – the "subor-
dinate officers" – Madison continued that "they are dependent on their superior,
he on the next superior, and he on whom? – on the senate" (Madison 1789). That
point reinforces the separation of powers when it comes to the creation and
administration of executive branch departments. The president, in short, is not
a chief executive with full removal powers of all government employees.

Early presidents through the administration of John Quincy Adams made
relatively few removals for cause (US Office of Personnel Management 2003).
By the Jackson administration, the spoils system began to take root, although
Jackson himself criticized the system. The 1832 party platform supporting his
reelection campaign said,

> The indiscriminate removal of public officers for a mere difference of polit-
> ical opinion is a gross abuse of power, and the doctrine boldly preached in the
> United States Senate, that to the victors belong the spoils of the vanquished, is
> detrimental to the interests, corrupting to the morals, and dangerous to the
> liberties of the country. (US Office of Personnel Management 2003, 20).

Moreover, although the Pendleton Act did not protect against the dismissal of
federal employees, it focused on solving the urgent problem of the day: enhancing
the government's capacity and ensuring that competence, not political favoritism,
determined federal hiring. Protections for civil servants gradually increased over
the years to something close to its modern form at the end of World War II.

If there is a dispute about the historical foundations of the modern civil
service, there is no dispute about the goals advanced by the conservatives. It
is a fundamental effort to reset the balance between the accountability and

competence of civil servants, strengthening the role of political executives by bringing experts under tighter control. That, the conservative activists contended, would break the back of the "deep state."

Trump's "Sharpiegate" episode demonstrates the risks of this approach, however. As Hurricane Dorian neared the east coast of the United States in September 2019, the president said that Alabama was one of the states likely to be affected. The National Weather Service forecast, however, showed the storm taking a different path. Trump continued to insist that he was right, however, and showed reporters a map of the projected storm track, on which someone had crudely used a thick pen to redraw the map to include Alabama. There was substantial political pressure on the National Oceanographic and Atmospheric Administration, of which the Weather Service was a part, to change its forecast to match the president's pronouncement, and two top political appointees issued a statement that seemed to support Trump.

A later investigation by the National Academy of Public Administration found that these efforts "compromised NOAA's integrity and reputation as an independent scientific agency" (Freedman and Samenow 2020). The inspector general of the Department of Commerce, which houses NOAA and the National Weather Service, was harshly critical of internal pressure on the Weather Service's Birmingham office to change its forecast. That pressure, the inspector general concluded, "could have a chilling effect on NWS forecasters' future public safety messages, as well as undercut public trust in NWS forecasts" (US Department of Commerce 2020, 2).

The "Sharpiegate" episode demonstrated the grave risks of political pressure designed to change expert judgment. Just what role should experts play – and to what degree should their expertise stand apart from politics? That is a puzzle intricately interwoven with the government's pursuit of its mission, especially as multiple social goals became layered on top of the basic quest to match the government's hiring to the skills needed to do the job.

8 Mission

Especially toward the end of the twentieth century, a wide variety of interest groups, from both the right and the left, pressed to use government hiring to pursue an equally wide array of objectives. There were policies for providing positions for veterans, advancing the interests of unions, promoting social goals like diversity, employing recent college graduates, or making statements about the importance of political symbols. Cutting government jobs became a tactic for shrinking the size of the government. But all these goals became enmeshed in the basic debate over the role of government experts.

The public service, of course, exists primarily to implement the government's policies. It ought to have neither more nor fewer employees than are needed to do that job and to do so with skill. The social objectives are truly important, of course, but they are secondary to the fundamental role of government experts: to do the government's work. Over time, however, these other objectives became marbled into the government's policies about the public service, to the point that they often dominated the system, loading it with conflicting objectives that sometimes blinded virtually everyone to the purposes it was created to serve.

There are deep historical roots for this debate. Since the time of the ancient Greeks, Chinese, and Romans, the central role of experts in government has been creating enough capacity to accomplish the government's mission. Creating jobs for loyalists, and using those jobs to cement loyalty, has always been an important element – and sometimes the dominant theme. But accomplishing the government's mission has always been the central reason for creating experts in the government's bureaucracy. That inevitably has established experts as a source of political power, which in turn has made them a target for those opposing the programs they administer. It is scarcely surprising, therefore, that attacking government workers becomes the focus of a proxy war over the government's size, purpose, and impact.

On the right, it became difficult – even impossible – to cut programs activists opposed. Cutting the number of government employees, which made it difficult – even impossible – to manage those programs well became the alternative. The Reagan administration made big cuts in the federal government's blue-collar employment. In 2016, House Republicans recommended cutting the pay of federal employees and requiring agencies to fill just two of every three vacancies. In 2022, Sen. Rick Scott (R-Fla.) proposed cutting the federal workforce by 25 percent and creating a twelve-year term limit on all federal employees. Then, in 2023, Democrats could not fight off a big cut in the IRS budget as the price for Republican support of an increase in the debt ceiling. For Republicans, public employees became the focus of cutting the size of government. If they could not slash programs, they could at least weaken the government's ability to deliver them.

On the left, interest groups sought to protect the number of federal employees and the unions that represented them. The Biden administration, for example, issued an executive order "dedicated to mobilizing the federal government's policies, programs, and practices to empower workers to organize and successfully bargain with their employers," including, of course, the government itself (2021). For Democrats, this signaled a shift to proceduralism, a large departure from what Bagley (2019, 349) called "a results-oriented, non-legalistic approach to administrative power" during the New Deal years.

The result of these assaults, from both the right and the left, has been a retreat away from the "substantial justice" for which Franklin D. Roosevelt had campaigned (Hinton 1940). Instead, the system moved toward "technical legalism," a shift from deciding what resources the government needed to accomplish its mission, set in law, toward fighting over procedure. The solution, as Bagley (2019, 400) contended, is this: "We should – indeed, we must – revive a strain of thinking that connects the legitimacy of the administrative state to its ability to satisfy public aspirations." How can government do the things that the people want to be done? And how can governments deal with one of the biggest challenges of the twenty-first century: restoring public trust in governmental institutions? And what happens to trust if government does not have the expertise it needs to do what the people want done?

Building Trust by Transforming the Public Service

This debate has reverberated through democracies around the world, especially in tackling the global problem of trust in government. The Finnish think tank, Demos, called for a global transformation of the civil service (2023). Meanwhile, McKinsey, the global management consulting firm, examined the role of public employees in Canada, France, Germany, Mexico, the United Kingdom, and the United States. It found that when public employees focus on delivering services more effectively, with an eye to improving the experience of the people, trust increased nine-fold, and employee morale increased by 50 percent (see Table 2). A personnel system focused on the mission – and on engaging employees to promote better results for the people – would vastly improve both the reality and the perception of the government's performance. More generally, the Organization for Economic Cooperation and Development (2022) found that the "government's capacity to address global and intergenerational issues" was a major driver in improving trust in government.

There is a large literature exploring how improved government performance can promote trust in government. That, in turn, depends on skilled employees who can deliver that performance (Bouckaert 2012; Jennings et al. 2021; Kettl 2017; Organization for Economic Cooperation and Development 2022). But that raises the deeper issue of why, if we know what to do, we do not do it more often. Shifting technology, moreover, has changed the way work gets done. In 2020, a report from the Society for Human Resource Management and Willis Towers Watson (2020), a consulting firm, concluded that "85 percent of jobs that will exist in 2030 have not been invented yet." The challenge of building the competence of government has never been greater because the pace of change has never been faster.

Table 2 Improved customer experience leads to increased trust

- Satisfied customers are nine times more like to trust the agency providing the service
- Satisfied customers are nine times more likely to agree that an agency is delivering on its mission
- Dissatisfied customers are two times more likely to reach out for help three or more times
- Dissatisfied customers are two times more likely to publicly express dissatisfaction
- Long-term organization success is 50 percent driven by organizational health and is mutually reinforced by customer experience

Source: D'Emidio et al. 2019.

The COVID-19 pandemic accelerated that change. More employees in the private sector – and in government as well – worked from home. David C. Wyld (2022) predicted that more work would be remote, and that organizations would need eight building blocks: ensuring the workers had the technical connections that they needed; promoting communications to link elements of the organization together; creating strategies to foster collaboration; managing – and maintaining – the organization's culture; developing the best oversight for the organization's workers; building the physical spaces that would support new ways of working; establishing management styles that create the compassion that remote workers would need; and devising strategic focus for the new methods of work. The Biden administration's Presidential Management Agenda (PMA), in fact, nudged federal agencies toward a fresh effort to rethink the government's human capital strategy:

> Federal agencies must attract, hire, develop, and empower talented individuals who are well suited and well prepared to face the challenges the Government faces, both in the near and long term. Agencies must also use what they have learned about the resilience and adaptability of the Federal workforce to make the Federal Government an ideal, modern, and forward-thinking employer. (Performance.gov 2023)

The PMA drove federal officials to rethink how best to recruit and motivate their employees to work in a twenty-first-century economy, one that not only was changing at lightning speed but one also where mega-shocks like COVID-19 accelerated change. For the government, that posed three enormous challenges.

First, in competing for talent, the government had to find ways of recruiting new employees with the skills needed for the mission defined in law.

The government found itself in a labor market where private employers offered their employees greater flexibility and exciting challenges. Digging ever deeper into existing people systems would only guarantee that the government would fall far behind its private partners. Second, the government needed to adapt its people systems to the changing skills the government needed, from data visualization to artificial intelligence to partnership management, in grants, contracts, and shared services. Matching those systems to the government's needs posed an enormous challenge for a personnel system that had barely changed in fifty years. Third, the government needed to navigate a political system that had come to view the civil service as a battleground for fighting out the big questions of government, from what government ought to do to how best to do it, that opposing sides could not – or would not – deal with directly.

Nongovernmental Experts Shape Government Policy

The fierce cross-currents of policy about the public service led American governments to sidestep the debate by relying far more on nongovernmental experts not only for implementing but also for shaping public policy. Private contractors provided far more management support, created information technology systems, and even drafted policies. The contracts provide the government with the flexibility to increase short-term capacity for new projects and to obtain expert advice that the government might not itself possess. For rapidly changing areas like IT, that is especially useful. But the contracts also provide workarounds to employment caps set by Congress and to inflexibilities created by the civil service system.

These service contracts also posed great risks, the US Government Accountability Office found. Federal agencies tended not to think strategically about how best to use these service contractors and, even more important, how to ensure that private contractors do not end up implicitly setting government policy. That, GAO concluded, "could put the government at risk of losing control of its mission if performed by contractors without proper oversight by government officials" (US Government Accountability Office 2020b). Many government agencies found it impossible to operate without a heavy reliance on service contractors for management support. But, on the other hand, the more the government relied on these contractors, the more it risked outsourcing the expertise it needed for effective and responsive governance.

The rise of artificial intelligence (AI) has sparked even more fundamental changes in the government's sources of expertise. AI has made it far easier to provide better customer service to the public and modernize many of the government's antiquated management systems. However, calls for government protection against abuses and potential dangers of AI have developed as fast as AI's innovations have grown. The government has struggled to develop expertise fast enough to keep up with these changes. The government's fragmentation, moreover, made it virtually impossible to establish a coordinated point of public leverage over the rapidly developing AI world. Expertise about AI – and, especially, AI's vast implications – is highly likely to rest with its private creators. So, too, are the strategies for implementing AI on the frontiers of technology.

These two mega-trends – contracting out expertise for delivering policy and for shaping it, and then struggling to govern the emerging AI realm – have shifted more of the reservoir of expertise on which government depends to private hands. That, in turn, has further increased the challenge of building the expertise government needs to govern in the twenty-first century to accomplish its mission – and to shift the government's personnel from symbols of political conflicts to engines for delivering the government's mission.

Making Mission Matter

Of course, governments have always been tempted to use the people who work for them to advance a host of other goals, from securing the emperor's rule in ancient China to pushing back on corporate power in nineteenth-century Britain. At the core, however, is the rule of law: how to develop the expertise needed to accomplish the government's mission. Government positions have always been attractive as sinecures. But mission always mattered most. Reagan's privatization agenda and Clinton's reinventing government both wobbled away from the mission, although both grew out of profound and serious efforts to redefine how the government could best do what it needed to do. In both cases, it became inevitable that bureaucrats became larger-than-life symbols of the government the presidents were seeking to reform.

If government is to solve the political tensions that surround the effort to balance capacity and control in the twenty-first century, the keystone must be reconnecting the government's capacity with the government's mission and focusing the government's employees on strengthening that capacity while maintaining accountability. It is the essential element in re-establishing the capacity of the state to do the people's business. As Brink Lindsey (2021) of the Niskanen Center put it, "Like beached fish suddenly appreciating the existence of water, we have come to recognize the crucial importance of state capacity because of shocks caused by its absence."

Five essential elements define the necessary steps to make mission matter. But as we will see in the next section, these elements are also incomplete.

1. *Making mission matter.* Amid the ideological and pragmatic battles since 1980 over the size and shape of the civil service, it is easy to forget the lessons from the nineteenth century: the purpose of the civil service is to implement the government's programs, with a high level of efficiency and in a way that is responsive to elected officials. Everything else, including the overwhelming push toward proceduralism and political symbols, is secondary. What matters is restoring the importance of mission in the debate over the civil service.

2. *Planning the connection between expertise and mission.* To accomplish the government's mission, it needs enough experts, with enough of the right expertise, to do so. Both the size and composition of the civil service depend on what it needs to do its job – and accomplish its mission. Even important intermediate goals, like veterans' preference, is secondary to the challenge of assessing the expertise the government needs. This, in turn demands far stronger strategic workforce planning, so the government knows where it is going and how to get there.

3. *Licensing flexibility and experimentation.* The government's mission is becoming increasingly complex. So, too, are the connections between the government and its nongovernmental partners, including its contractors. In such an environment, no one-size-fits-all approach can work. Moreover, any agency that seeks to root itself deeply in the past will be unable to adapt to the future. Agencies need the flexibility to experiment with new strategies for accomplishing their missions. Experimentation, not regimentation, ought to shape the future.

4. *Developing metrics to assess success.* Of equal importance is assessing which experiments work – and which ones do not. Agencies need additional flexibility in their human capital practices. Guiding that flexibility by developing evidence about what works best is key.

5. *Re-emphasizing the fundamental importance of merit.* Different agencies need to manage their workforce differently to accomplish their different goals. But all that work needs to proceed under the broad umbrella of the merit system. The fundamental principles of the merit system endure: hiring on the basis of each employee's expertise in pursuing the agency's mission; protection against political interference in that work; and a shield against dismissal because of political favoritism (see Table 3). This does not mean, of course, that employees can disconnect from assessments of their own performance. Indeed, good performance ought to be rewarded, and poor performers ought to be removed. But the fundamental merit principles ought to endure.

Table 3 Merit system principles

1. Recruit qualified individuals from all segments of society; conduct fair and open competition; select and advance employees based solely on merit.
2. Treat employees and applicants fairly and equitably, with proper regard for their privacy and constitutional rights.
3. Provide equal pay for work of equal value and recognize excellent performance.
4. Maintain high standards of integrity, conduct, and concern for the public interest.
5. Manage employees efficiently and effectively.
6. Address inadequate performance fairly and decisively and separate poor performers, as appropriate.
7. Educate and train employees to improve individual and organizational performance.
8. Protect employees against favoritism, political coercion and arbitrary action and prohibit abuse of authority.
9. Protect employees against reprisal for the lawful disclosure of information that is reasonably believed to evidence: (1) a violation of any law, rule, or regulation; or (2) mismanagement, a gross waste of funds, an abuse of authority, or a substantial and specific danger to public health or safety.

Adapted from Title 5, United States Code, Section 2301(b). US Merit Systems Protection Board (2020), www.mspb.gov/studies/studies/The_Merit_System_Principles_Keys_to_ Managing_the_Federal_Workforce_1371890.pdf

To these five elements we can add the sixth essential, overarching imperative: ensuring that government's experts are accountable for how they exercise that power. That echoes the big questions with which the Element began, and we turn to the multiple dimensions of this challenge in the last section.

9 Accountability

Governments have learned since ancient times that political leaders cannot govern for long without experts – and that government's expertise works best within a bureaucratic structure designed to create and then control that expertise. The more complex social forces and public policies become, the more the government needs experts. But with more expertise comes greater power and a growing challenge for holding it to account. The greater the challenge in controlling experts, the more these become lightning rods for society's biggest political tensions.

For millennia, governments have struggled to find the right balance between building competence and asserting control. That balance has always been dynamic. For the United States and for nations around the world, the twenty-first century has brought growing worries. How best can governments build the expertise they need to provide effective public services without feeding a beast that threatens to escape the control of top officials – and the people? This puzzle has become the central issue for democracies.

The Quest for Balance in Controlling Experts

In the United States, that puzzle has always built on the rise of experts in the executive branch and then the balance between the executive and legislative branches of government. The nation's founders worried from the beginning that by throwing off one powerful executive they would fall prey to another. The founders crafted a solution by bookending presidential powers (in Article II of the Constitution) between a strong legislature (in Article I) and the judicial branch (in Article III).

Congress, however, has undermined its own power through partisan gridlock and ineffective oversight. By the early twenty-first century, the problem had become so bad that Thomas E. Mann and Norman J. Ornstein (2006) called Congress "the broken branch" of government. They soon declared that the problem was "even worse than it looks" (Mann and Ornstein 2012). The founders might have intended Congress to be the "first branch of government," but by the 2020s Congress became virtually immobilized.

Expanding executive power filled the vacuum created by congressional polarization. That, in turn, led to worries that enhanced presidential power might drift toward authoritarianism. Over the world's history, the prime tool of authoritarian regimes has always been a strong collection of experts within powerful bureaucracies. That, in fact, fed the modern incarnation of the "deep state" in Turkey, as we saw in Section 1.

Liberals have long sought an activist government, but in twenty-first-century American politics, there has been surprising support among conservatives to shift the balance toward executive power. As we saw in Section 7, the case for Schedule F rested on the foundation of a "unitary executive" theory, an approach that echoed the debates at the constitutional convention, where the founders defined the structure of presidential power. Hamilton was the perennial champion of the executive. In Federalist 70, he made his famous case for "energy in the executive." "A feeble Executive implies a feeble execution of the government. A feeble execution is but another phrase for a bad execution; and a government ill executed, whatever it may be in theory, must be, in practice, a bad government," Hamilton wrote. To create the energy he thought that the executive needed, he contended, "The ingredients which constitute energy in the Executive are, first, unity; secondly, duration; thirdly, an adequate provision for its support; fourthly, competent powers."

There's a profound irony, of course, that even some of Hamilton's opponents became Hamiltonians on taking office. Thomas Jefferson had strongly argued against Hamilton's approach to presidential power. As president, however, he relied on the implied powers of the presidency to justify the Louisiana Purchase and double the size of the country. But just how much power should the president have over the executive branch's experts? And how much power should the president have over firing career experts who are either poor performers or insufficiently loyal? The answer to that question developed gradually over time, especially with the creation of the merit system. In 1926, the Supreme Court decided in *Myers v. United States* that the president could remove the officers he appoints (272 US 52 [1926]). In later cases, including *Humphrey's Executor v. United States* (295 US 602 [1935]) and *Morrison v. Olson* (487 US 654, 685–93 [1988]), the Court established limits on the president's removal power, holding that in some circumstances appointees could only be removed for cause.

However, in the early twenty-first century, the Court began drifting toward the "unitary executive" position, especially on the Roberts Court. In 2020, the Court held, "In our constitutional system, the executive power belongs to the President, and that power generally includes the ability to supervise and remove the agents who wield executive power in his stead." (*Seila Law LLC v. CFPB*, No. 19-7, slip op. at 26 [US June 29, 2020]). Indeed, conservatives suggested, if civil servants were impediments to presidential leadership, their power ought to be reduced. And if public employee unions constrained the executive's power, as conservative critics often contended, those groups might even be unconstitutional (Howard 2023). Given the fierce political battles around these issues, the roots of these debates remain as lively as they were for the founders – or in the echoes of the puzzles across the ages.

It has long been tempting for government critics to contend that chief executives in the government ought to have the power of private sector executives: to dismiss employees at will. But the president is not a CEO, with Congress as the board of directors. Rather, the government is a unique institution charged with discovering and advancing the public interest, with the power to do so split between three branches of government. The private-sector CEO debate tends to obscure the underlying tensions that the founders deliberately build into the American constitutional system – and the shifting patterns of power between the branches that have developed over time and that never will be settled.

Executive power in the United States has a base not only in the Constitution but also in the rule of law, which flows from a sharing of responsibility. The laws presidents are charged with faithfully executing, the organizations they manage, the money they spend, and the people public organizations employ are all the product of ongoing legislative decisions. Government experts thus find themselves constantly in a tug of war between presidents seeking to have them do their bidding and a Congress that wants to shape their role and behavior, in a tug that never tires.

The conservatives of the late twentieth century, like Ronald Reagan, Barry Goldwater, William F. Buckley, Jr., and George Will, argued tirelessly for a smaller government within the framework of balanced constitutional powers. The conservatives of the early twenty-first century, in contrast, made the case for a stronger president with more power over the career employees of the executive branch establishment. There is thus a deep division between the two brands of conservatism. During the Trump administration, for example, adviser James Sherk proposed what he called "the 'Constitutional Option' for firing federal employees." He wrote that "there are legal arguments that Article II executive power gives the president inherent authority to dismiss any federal employee. This implies civil service legislation and union contracts impeding that authority are unconstitutional" (Sherk 2017). Just how far does the president's power go in removing administrators who administer laws passed by Congress in agencies created by Congress? Just who is accountable to whom for what?

Accountability and Politics in Twenty-First-Century America

This debate is not only about the essential question of how best the civil service ought to provide the government with the capacity it needs. It goes right to the heart of the rule of law in the American republic, and how the republic ought to structure the role of experts.

Since ancient Rome and China, there has been a constant search for a rule of law to find the balance between the creation of government capacity and the need to control the power that experts inevitably employ. In the United States, especially since the 1980s, there has been a rising ideological debate about how best to resolve this issue – and to control the power of experts. That, in turn, sets the stage for as fundamental a debate about the separation of powers – indeed about the American constitutional system – as the county has seen since its founding. Four increasingly fundamental questions about American democracy shape this debate:

1. *What should be the balance between executive and legislative power in policy implementation?* Society's problems have become increasingly complex and solving them has depended increasingly on more experts. A stronger role for experts, however, also creates greater executive power that is harder to hold accountable. How can legislators hold these experts accountable on issues that are increasingly difficult to penetrate by non-experts?

2. *How much loyalty should chief executives expect from their career experts?*
   The rising power of these experts also challenges the ability of top executives to control them. Few things frustrate elected officials more than discovering that they cannot advance their policy goals without the government's career experts – and that the experts do not move fast enough, or prove insufficiently loyal, to put their ideas in place quickly. Of course, the more complex a problem, the longer it takes to do it: navigating the requirements of the law, dealing with the inevitable technical issues, and putting new administrative systems into place. To elected officials, that can look like policy sabotage (and, indeed, sometimes it is). But charging ahead without carefully laying the groundwork can pave the path to policy ruin. How can elected officials and their political appointees move fast, within the law and within the technical constraints of their policy ideas?

3. *How much expertise should government build within its own bureaucracy, and how much can – and should – the government contract out expertise?*
   The rise of government contractors in the twentieth century, especially contracts for professional services not only to deliver but also to help make policy, has often pushed aside the government's own experts. That, in turn, has pushed more public policy into private hands. And, from the point of view of elected officials, it made government seem even less malleable and controllable. Reliance on these contractors has become an inescapable element of the government's network of experts, but how can these third parties be held accountable for the nature of their work?

4. *What should be the role of the government's central personnel agency?*
   Within the framework of the civil service system, there has been a constant tug between agency heads, who want flexibility in managing their programs, and the central office (most recently the Office of Personnel Management, at the federal level) that is charged with ensuring uniform policies across the government. Political support for that central role has eroded in the face of the need of operating officials for flexibility; the quest for flexibility has eroded the merit system principles that guided American policy for more than a century. Just what should be the balance between that central control and operating flexibility? What merit system principles should guide government policy into the twenty-first century?

The case of Dr. Anthony Fauci during the COVID-19 crisis underlines this point. On his retirement in 2022, he shared advice for young scientists in the federal government. He urged them to "stick with the science, stick with the evidence, stick with the public health issues and stay out of politics" (Bublé 2022). That, of course, is impossible, because COVID-19 demonstrated the eternal truth: expertise is inevitably embedded in politics. Every significant decision about COVID-19 had deep political implications and therefore rested on political as well as technical judgments: whether to encourage the wearing of masks, whether to open schools, whether to adopt mandates for the public's action, or whether to encourage vaccinations, among many other puzzles.

As Aaron Wildavsky wrote, if we are to understand the true meaning of public policy, "we must first exorcize the ghost of rationality, which haunts the house of public policy" (Wildavsky 2018, 5). Expertise is inherently political. Any effort to promote any course of action, based on the notion that the experts have relied on their expertise, is flawed. Every bit of expertise inevitably makes some assumptions and pushes away others, relies on some data and not others because no one can ever know everything, and favors, even if implicitly, one course of action over others.

The role of experts is inevitably political because expertise inescapably hinges on the values of those who offer expertise and of those who receive it. The political tensions woven into this issue, moreover, have often shifted over time, because of a series of forces:

- *Personal loyalty to the executive.* Government jobs have always been attractive and, therefore, it has always been tempting to treat them as sinecures from which executives expect fealty. American presidents have long used appointments to ambassadorial positions, for example, as rewards for political support. During the Trump administration, White House officials interviewed political officials in what appointees called "loyalty tests" to discover and eliminate leaks (Diamond, Lippman, and Cook 2020).
- *The policy goals of the executive.* Presidents believe that elections ought to have consequences, especially in translating their policy goals into accomplishments. Presidents and their staffs tend to view anything less than immediate action as opposition. Sometimes that is the case. Sometimes that is because experts are torn by other accountability goals.
- *The merit principles within the civil service system.* Career experts jealously guard the securities that the system provides. Presidents often complain that they cannot dismiss poor performers or administrators who slow-walk their policies. But more than a century's efforts to define and protect the civil service have created barriers to presidential pressure on experts.
- *The professional norms that accompany expert training.* Career experts believe that their job is to use their skills to translate policies into results. Presidents criticize experts for hiding behind technical judgments, but presidents frequently want things that are far more complicated than they often recognize. An old joke among government officials is that there are two ways

of sabotaging a new executive's policies: to do nothing that they are asked to do – and to do everything they are asked to do. As Barack Obama discovered with the failed launch of his landmark health insurance program, failing to manage the details can undermine broad goals.

• *Compliance with the law.* The law is often ambiguous and subject to constant redefinition, conflict, and controversy. Experts often – rightly – point out that presidents might want one thing, but laws passed by Congress might direct them to do something else. In the American system, the president is the titular head of the federal bureaucracy, but its structure, budget, processes, and programs are defined by legislative action. The accountability of experts is therefore almost always divided between competing institutions. Legislation typically has islands of ambiguity, which allows different players to interpret the same legislative wording in different ways. That frequently brings in the courts. Government experts therefore often find themselves in the middle of a three-way tug over how they ought to do their work.

Everyone seeks accountability, but what they mean by it often could not be more different. Moreover, what the players in the political system believe accountability means often changes over time, as the balance of political power shifts.

Expertise is political. It always has been, always will be, and always should be, because expertise inevitably is about political values and how societies pursue them. Indeed, that is the fundamental conclusion of this Element. The question has always been about how best to structure the role of expertise, how much power experts have, and how best to control them. If experts assert that they are pursuing science, those who disagree with them tend to conclude that the experts are unresponsive and out of control. If, on the other hand, elected officials insist on loyalty, experts cannot fully make use of their expertise, and policy outcomes inevitably suffer.

That is why the exercise of expertise is inescapably a political act. Political decisions only gain their meaning through the exercise of expertise. Finding the balance between control and capacity are eternal issues in governance. That tension has only become sharper in modern democracy, and finding the new balance has quietly become the most important dilemma for American governance in the middle third of the twenty-first century.

References

Anonymous (2018). "I Am Part of the Resistance inside the Trump Administration." *New York Times* (September 5), www.nytimes.com/2018/09/05/opinion/trump-white-house-anonymous-resistance.html.

Appleby, P. H. (1949). *Policy and Administration.* Tuscaloosa: University of Alabama Press.

Arnold, P. (2007)."The Brownlow Committee, Regulation, and the Presidency: Seventy Years Later." *Public Administration Review* 67:6 (November–December), 1030–1040.

Arthur, C. A. (1881). "First Annual Message: December 6, 1881." Charlottesville: Miller Center, University of Virginia, https://millercenter.org/the-presidency/presidential-speeches/december-6-1881-first-annual-message.

Arthur, C. A. (1884). "Fourth Annual Message: December 1, 1884." Charlottesville: Miller Center, University of Virginia, https://millercenter.org/the-presidency/presidential-speeches/december-1-1884-fourth-annual-message.

Ashworth, J. (2021). "Ancient Britons Adapted to Drink Milk a Millennium Earlier Than Europeans." *National History Museum* (December 22), www.nhm.ac.uk/discover/news/2021/december/britons-adapted-to-drink-milk-millennium-earlier-than-Europeans.html.

Austin Water (2022a). "Austin Water Releases Investigation Report into Boil Water Notice" (March 29), www.austintexas.gov/news/austin-water-releases-investigation-report-boil-water-notice.

Austin Water (2022b). "Investigation Report Summary" (March 22), https://austintexas.gov/edims/pio/document.cfm?id=379790.

Autullo, R. (2022). "Amid Boil Notice Fallout, Departing Director Says Austin Water Faces Staff and Culture Problems." *Austin American-Statesman* (February 15), www.statesman.com/story/news/2022/02/15/city-austin-boil-water-notice-staffing-culture-issues-departing-director-says/6799190001/.

Bagley, N. (2019). "The Procedure Fetish." *Michigan Law Review* 118:3, 345–401.

Baldi, D. (2010). "Il Codex Florentinus del Digesto e il 'Fondo Pandette' della Biblioteca Laurenziana (con un'appendice di documenti inediti)." *Segno e testo* 8, 99–186.

Barr, S. (2001). "Opinions Fly on Civil Service Job Protection and Hiring Red Tape." *Washington Post* (November 5), www.washingtonpost.com/archive/local/2001/11/05/opinions-fly-on-civil-service-job-protection-and-hiring-red-tape/988da489-ee33-4bb5-8334-5b03b20b76bb/.

Barrie, J. (2018). "Royal Butler Finally Settles Tea or Milk First Debate – and Reveals Queen's Favourite Blend." *Mirror* (March 23), www.mirror.co.uk/3am/celebrity-news/royal-butler-finally-settles-tea-12238061.

Bendix, R. (1945). "Bureaucracy and the Problem of Power." *Public Administration Review* 5:3 (summer), 194–209.

Berhnardt, D. L. (2023). *You Report to Me: Accountability for the Failing Administrative State*. New York: Encounter Books.

Bouckaert, G. (2012). "Trust and Public Administration." *Administration*, 60:1, 91–115.

Brian Resnick, B. (2015). "This Is the Brain That Shot President James Garfield." *The Atlantic* (October 4), www.theatlantic.com/politics/archive/2015/10/this-is-the-brain-that-shot-president-james-garfield/454212/.

Brownlow, L. (1958). *A Passion for Anonymity: The Autobiography of Louis Brownlow*. Chicago: University of Chicago Press.

Bublé, C. (2022). "Fauci's Farewell: His Legacy, The New Booster and Forthcoming Congressional Oversight." *GovExec* (November 23), www.govexec.com/management/2022/11/faucis-farewell-legacy-booster-forthcoming-congressional-oversight/380136/.

Carpenter, D. P. (2001). *The Forging of Bureaucratic Autonomy: Reputations, Networks, and Policy Innovation in Executive Agencies, 1862–1928*. Princeton: Princeton University Press.

Carter, J. (1978). "Civil Service Reform Act of 1978 Memorandum From the President" (November 8). www.presidency.ucsb.edu/documents/civil-service-reform-act-1978-memorandum-from-the-president.

Centre for Public Impact (2016). *Deliverology: The Science of Delivery* (April 6). www.centreforpublicimpact.org/insights/deliverology-science.

Chaucer, G. (1391, 2004). *A Treatise on the Astrolabe*. Chicago: University of Chicago Press.

Churchill, W. (1902). "Letter, 17 November." In H. Perkin (2002). *The Rise of Professional Society: England Since 1880*. London: Routledge, 169.

Citizens Committee for the Hoover Report (1955). *Digests and Analyses of the Nineteen Hoover Commission Reports*. Washington, DC: Citizens Committee for the Hoover Report (February).

"Civil Service History" (n.d.). www.civilservant.org.uk/misc-history.html.

Coase, R. H. (1976). "Adam Smith's View of Man." *The Journal of Law and Economics* 19:3 (October), 529–546.

Coolican, M. (2018). *No Tradesmen and No Women: The Origins of the British Civil Service*. London: Biteback Publishing.

Cormacain, R. (2022). *The Form of Legislation and the Rule of Law*. Oxford: Hart Publishing.

Corpus Juris Civilis (1606). https://catalog.hathitrust.org/api/volumes/oclc/23623638.html.

Coughlan, S. (2013). "Teachers in China Given Highest Level of Public Respect." *BBC News* (October 14), www.bbc.com/news/education-24381946.

Creel, H. G. (1964). "The Beginnings of Bureaucracy in China: The Origin of the Hsien." *Journal of Asian Studies* 23:2 (February), 155–184.

Cullen, T. W. (1986). "Most Federal Workers Need Only Be Competent." *Wall Street Journal* (May 21), 32.

Cunningham, E., T. Saich, and J. Turiel. (2020). "Understanding CCP Resilience: Surveying Chinese Public Opinion through Time." Cambridge, MA: Ash Center for Democratic Governance and Innovation, Harvard Kennedy School, https://ash.harvard.edu/publications/understanding-ccp-resilience-surveying-chinese-public-opinion-through-time.

D'Emdio, T., S. Greenberg, K. Heidenreich, J. Klier, J. Wagner, and T. Weber. (2019). "The Global Case for Customer Experience in Government." *McKinsey Insights* (September 10), www.mckinsey.com/industries/public-and-social-sector/our-insights/the-global-case-for-customer-experience-in-government.

Dean, J. (1971). "Dealing with our Political Enemies." Confidential memorandum (August 16), https://upload.wikimedia.org/wikipedia/commons/9/94/Dean-enemies-1.jpg.

Demos. (2023). "A New Ethos for the Civil Service" (June 1). https://demoshelsinki.fi/civil-service/.

Devine, D., D. D. Kirk, and P. Dans. (2023). "Central Personnel Agencies: Managing the Bureaucracy." In P. Dans and S. Groves, eds., *Mandate for Leadership: The Conservative Promise*. Washington, DC: Heritage Foundation, 69–85.

Diamond, D., D. Lippman, and N. Cook. (2020). "Trump Team Launches a Sweeping Loyalty Test to Shore Up Its Defenses." *Politico* (July 20), www.politico.com/news/2020/07/15/trump-appointees-loyalty-interviews-364616.

Dunleavy, P. (1985). "Bureaucrats, Budgets and the Growth of the State: Reconstructing an Instrumental Model." *British Journal of Political Science*, 15:3, 299–323.

Eggers, W. D., and D. F. Kettl. (2023). *Bridgebuilders: How Government Can Transcend Boundaries to Solve Big Problems*. Cambridge, MA: Harvard Business Review Press.

Elledge, J. (2022). "Don't Fall for Boris Johnson's "Deep State" Conspiracy Theory." *The New Statesman* (July 20), www.newstatesman.com/quickfire/ 2022/07/boris-johnsons-deep-state-conspiracy-theory.

Elman, B. A. (2009). "Civil Service Examinations." *Berkshire Encyclopedia of China: Modern and Historic Views of the World's Newest And Oldest Global Power*. Great Barrington, MA: Berkshire Publishing Group, 405–410, www .princeton.edu/~elman/documents/Civil%20Service%20Examinations.pdf

Everett, E., and M. Welch. (2023). "Let's Think Differently about Firing Poor Performers." *PM Magazine* (July 1), https://icma.org/articles/pm-magazine/ lets-think-differently-about-firing-poor-performers.

Flavelle, C., and B. Bain. (2017). "Bureaucrats Are Quietly Working to Undermine Trump's Agenda." *Bloomberg* (December 17), www.bloom berg.com/news/features/2017-12-18/washington-bureaucrats-are-chipping- away-at-trump-s-agenda?leadSource=uverify%20wall.

Foley, M. P. (2009). *The Catholic Contribution to Western Law*. Kirland, WA: Catholic Education Resource Center, www.catholiceducation.org/en/culture/ catholic-contributions/the-catholic-contribution-to-western-law.html.

Freedman, A., and J. Samenow. (2020). "NOAA Leaders Violated Agency's Scientific Integrity Policy, Hurricane Dorian 'Sharpiegate' Investigation Finds." *Washington Post* (June 15), www.washingtonpost.com/weather/ 2020/06/15/noaa-investigation-sharpiegate/.

Fukuyama, F. (2011). *The Origins of Political Order: From Prehuman Times to the French Revolution*. New York: Farrar, Straus and Giroux.

Funk, C., A. Tyson, G. Pasquini, and A. Spencer. (2022). "Americans Reflect on Nation's COVID-19 Response" (July 7). Washington, DC: Pew Research Center,www.pewresearch.org/science/2022/07/07/americans-reflect-on- nations-covid-19-response/.

Gabriel, R. A. (2009). *Thutmose III: The Military Biography of Egypt's Greatest Warrior King*. Washington, DC: Potomac Books.

Gibbon, E. (1952). *The Decline and Fall of the Roman Empire*. New York: Viking.

Goodnow, F. J. (1900). *Politics and Administration: A Study in Government*. New York: Russell and Russell.

Grace Commission (US Private Sector Survey on Cost Control) (1984). *Report*, www.google.com/url?sa=t&rct=j&q=&esrc=s&source=web&cd=&ved=2ah UKEwiA7ezjkqr9AhVwnGoFHRH4A2AQFnoECBYQAQ&url=https%3A %2F%2Fdigital.library.unt.edu%2Fark%3A%2F67531%2Fmetacrs9044%

2Fm1%2F1%2Fhigh_res_d%2FIP0281G.pdf&usg=AOvVaw35EEmzaA4h2
yFi4itt2DRh.

Graham, L. (2022). Tweet (January 26), https://twitter.com/lindseygrahamsc/
status/1486399049527869440.

Gulick, L. and L. Urwick. (1937). *Papers on the Science of Administration*.
New York: Institute of Public Administration.

HM Treasury (1949). *A Handbook for the New Civil Servant*. London: HM
Treasury, https://www.civilservant.org.uk/library/1949-HMT-A_Handbook_
for_the_New_Civil_Servant.pdf.

Halberstam, D. (1972). *The Best and the Brightest*. New York: Random House.

Han, Y. (1946). "The Chinese Civil Service: Yesterday and Today." *Pacific
Historical Review* 15:2 (June), 158–170.

Hartmann, B. (2020. *The Scribes of Rome: A Cultural and Social History of the
Scribae*. Cambridge: Cambridge University Press.

Heclo, H. (1999). "OMB and Neutral Competence." In J. P. Pfiffner, ed. *The
Managerial Presidency*. College Station: Texas A&M University Press.

Hinton, H. B. (1940). "House Sustains President's Veto of Agencies Bill."
New York Times (December 19), 1.

Hood, C. (1998). *The Art of the State: Culture, Rhetoric, and Public
Management*. Oxford: Clarendon Press.

Howard, P. K. (2023). *Not ACCOUNTABLE: Rethinking the Constitutionality
of Public Employee Unions*. Garden City, NY: Rodin Books.

Hunt, K. (2023). "Mystery of Why Roman Buildings Have Survived So Long
Has Been Unraveled, Scientists Say." *CNN Style* (January 6), www.cnn.com/
style/article/roman-concrete-mystery-ingredient-scn/index.html.

Ingraham, P. W. (2006). "Building Bridges over Troubled Waters: Merit as a
Guide." *Public Administration Review* 66:4 (July–August), 486–495.

Ingraham, P. W., and D. Rosenbloom. (1990). *The State of Merit in the Federal
Government*. Washington, DC: The National Commission on the Public
Service.

Interagency Veterans Advisory Council (2021). *The Status of Veterans in the
Federal Workforce* (November 11). Washington, DC: Interagency Veterans
Advisory Council, https://cdn.govexec.com/media/gbc/docs/pdfs_edit/
111021-cb1a.pdf.

IPSOS (2020). "More Than 1 in 3 Americans Believe a 'deep State' is Working
to Undermine Trump." *IPSOS* (December 30), www.ipsos.com/en-us/news-
polls/npr-misinformation-123020.

Jennings, W. et Al. (2021), "How Trust, Mistrust and Distrust Shape the
Governance of the COVID- 19 Crisis," *Journal of European Public Policy*,
28:8, 1174–1196. http://dx.doi.org/10.1080/13501763.2021.1942151.

Kamarck, E. (2013). "Lessons for the Future of Government Reform." Washington, DC: Brookings Institution, www.brookings.edu/testimonies/lessons-for-the-future-of-government-reform/.

Katz, E. (2018). "The Federal Government Has Gotten Slower at Hiring New Employees for 5 Consecutive Years." *GovExec.com* (March 1), www.govexec.com/management/2018/03/federal-government-has-gotten-slower-hiring-new-employees-five-consecutive-years/146348/.

Kellaway, L. (2013). "The Ancient Chinese Exam that Inspired Modern Job Recruitment." *BBC* (July 23), https://www.bbc.com/news/magazine-23376561.

Kennedy, B., A. Tyson, and C. Funk. (2022). "Americans' Trust in Scientists, Other Groups Declines." Washington, DC: Pew Research Center, www.pewresearch.org/science/2022/02/15/americans-trust-in-scientists-other-groups-declines/

Kettl, D. F. (2015). "Scott Walker's Real Legacy." *Washington Monthly* (June 7), https://washingtonmonthly.com/2015/06/07/scott-walkers-real-legacy/.

Kettl, D. F. (2017). *Can Governments Earn Our Trust?* Cambridge: Polity Press.

King, L. W. (n.d.). *The Code of Hammurabi*. New Haven: The Avalon Project, Yale Law School, https://avalon.law.yale.edu/ancient/hamframe.asp.

Lehner, U. (2015). "Catholic Theology and the Enlightenment (1670–1815)." Milwaukee: Marquette Univrersity Department of Theology, https://epublications.marquette.edu/cgi/viewcontent.cgi?article=1537&context=theo_fac.

Leich, H. H. (1953). "The Hoover Commission's Personnel Recommendations: A Progress Report." *American Political Science Review* 47:1 (March), 100–125.

Leung, B. (2018). "Teachers in China Are the World's Most Respected." *China Daily* (November 10), www.chinadaily.com.cn/a/201811/10/WS5be62f9ea310eff303287c6d.html.

Lewis, D. E. (2010). *The Politics of Presidential Appointments: Political Control and Bureaucratic Performance*. Princeton: Princeton University Press.

Li, F. (2013). *Early China: A Social and Cultural History*. Cambridge: Cambridge University Press.

Lindsey, B. (2021). "State Capacity: What is it, How We Lost it, and How to Get it Back." (November 18), www.niskanencenter.org/state-capacity-what-is-it-how-we-lost-it-and-how-to-get-it-back/.

Lowe, R. (2011). *The Official History of the British Civil Service, Reforming the Civil Service*, vol. 1, *The Fulton Years 1966-81*. London: Routledge.

Macpherson, C. B. (1962). *The Political Theory of Possessive Individualism: Hobbes to Locke*. Oxford: Clarendon Press.

Madison, J. (1789). "Removal Power of the President" (June 17), https:// founders.archives.gov/documents/Madison/01-12-02-0143.

Mann, T. E., and N. J. Ornstein. (2006). *The Broken Branch: How Congress Is Failing America and How to Get It Back on Track*. New York: Oxford University Press.

Mann, T. E., and N. J. Ornstein. (2012). *It's Even Worse Than It Looks: How the American Constitutional System Collided with the New Politics of Extremism*. New York: Basic Books.

Markmanellis (2017). "'Milk in First': A Miffy Question" (History of Tea Project at Queen Mary University of London, May 11), https://qmhistoryof tea.wordpress.com/2017/05/11/milk-in-first-a-miffy-question/.

Matthews, K. D. (1970). "Roman Aqueducts: Technical Aspects of Their Construction." *Penn Museum: Expedition*, 13:1, www.penn.museum/sites/ expedition/roman-aqueducts/#:~:text=With%20an%20average%20gradient %20of,the%20hilltops%20of%20the%20city.

McGlinchy, A. (2022). "Here's What We Know about What Caused Last Week's Boil-Water Notice in Austin." *KUT.org* (February 15), www.kut .org/austin/2022-02-15/heres-what-we-know-about-what-caused-last-weeks-boil-water-notice-in-austin.

McSweeney, T. J., and M. K. Spike. (2015). *The Significance of the Corpus Juris Civilis: Matilda of Canossa and the Revival of Roman Law*. Williamsburg, VA: College of William and Mary Law School.

Millard, C. (2011). *Destiny of the Republic: A Tale of Madness, Medicine, and the Murder of a President*. New York: Anchor Books.

Montjoy R. S., and D. J. Watson. (1995). "A Case for Reinterpreted Dichotomy of Politics and Administration as a Professional Standard in Council-Manager Government." *Public Administration Review* 55:3 (May/ June), 231.

Mosher, F. C. (1968). *Democracy and the Public Service*. New York: Oxford University Press.

National Academy of Public Administration (2017). *No Time to Wait: Building a Public Service for the 21st Century*. (July). Washington, DC: National Academy of Public Administration, https://napawash.org/academy-studies/ no-time-to-wait-part-2-building-a-public-service-for-the-21st-century.

Naval (2021). Tweet (August 14), https://twitter.com/naval/status/ 1426745940577198082.

Niskanen, W. A. (1971). *Bureaucracy and Representative Goernment*. Chicago: Aldine, Atherton.

"Nixon's Revolutionary Vision for American Governance" (2017). Nixon Today (January 24), www.nixonfoundation.org/2017/01/nixons-vision-for-american-governance/.

Northcote, S. H., and C. E. Trevelyan. (1854). *Report on the Organisation of the Permanent Civil Service*. London: Presented to both Houses of Parliament by Command of Her Majesty, www.civilservant.org.uk%2Flibrary%2F1854_Northcote_Trevelyan_Report.pdfC.

Norton E. Long, N. E. (1954). "Public Policy and Administration: The Goals of Rationality and Responsibility." *Public Administration Review* 14:1 (Winter), 22.

Nozick, R. (1974). *Anarchy, State, and Utopia*. New York: Basic Books.

NPR. (2010). "Who Oversees Homeland Security? Um, Who Doesn't?" (July 20), www.npr.org/templates/story/story.php?storyId=128642876.

Oliveira, E., G. Abner, S. Lee, K. Suzuki, H. Hur, and J. L. Perry. (2023). "What Does the Evidence Tell Us about Merit Principles and Government Performance?" *Public Administration*, 1–23.

Organization for Economic Cooperation and Development (2022). "Trust in Government." www.oecd.org/governance/trust-in-government.

"Pendleton Act (1883)," www.ourdocuments.gov/doc.php?flash=false&doc=48.

Peng, P. (2018). "War, Bureaucracy, and State Capacity: Evidence from Imperial China." Durham, NC: Duke University, https://sites.duke.edu/statecapacity/files/2019/04/Peng-2019-War-Bureaucracy-State-Capacity-in-China.pdf.

Performance.gov. (2023). "President's Management Agenda: Strengthening and Empowering the Federal Workforce," www.performance.gov/pma/workforce/.

Peters, E. N. (n.d.). *CanonLaw.info*, http://canonlaw.info/

Plato (n.d.). *The Republic*, www.gutenberg.org/files/1497/1497-h/1497-h.htm

Portillo, S., N. Humphrey, and D. Bearfield. (2022). *The Myth of Bureaucratic Neutrality: An Examination of Merit and Representation*. New York: Routledge.

President's Committee on Administrative Management (1937). *Report of the President's Committee: Administrative Management in the Government of the United States*. Washington, DC: US Government Printing Office, https://babel.hathitrust.org/cgi/pt?id=mdp.39015030482726&view=1up&seq=4.

Pressman, J. L., and A. Wildavsky. (1973) *How Great Expectations in Washington Are Dashed in Oakland; Or, Why It's Amazing that Federal Programs Work at All, This Being a Saga of the Economic Development Administration as Told by Two Sympathetic Observers Who Seek to Build*

Morals on a Foundation of Ruined Hopes. Berkeley: University of California Press.

Provis, C. (2019). "Confucianism, Virtue, and Wisdom." In A. J. G. Sison, G. R. Beabout, and I. Ferrero, eds., *Handbook of Virtue Ethics in Business and Management*. Dordrecht: Springer Netherlands, 425–434.

Rauch, J. D. (1995). *Demosclerosis: The Silent Killer of American Government*. New York: Three Rivers Press.

Reagan, R. (1986). "News Conference" (August 12). Simi Valley, CA: Ronald Reagan Presidential Foundation and Institute, www.reaganfoundation.org/ronald-reagan/reagan-quotes-speeches/news-conference-1/.

Report of the Proceedings in the Case of the United States vs. Charles J. Guiteau, Tried in the Supreme Court of the District of Columbia, Holding a Criminal Term, and Beginning November 14, 1881, Part II. (1882). Washington, DC: Government Printing Office.

Roberts, A. (1996). "Why the Brownlow Committee Failed: Neutrality and Partisanship in the Early Years of Public Administration." *Administration and Society* 28:1, 3–38.

Roberts, J. M. (2019). "Brazil's Bolsonaro Should Follow Trump's Lead and Slash Regulations." *Heritage Foundation* (November 26), www.heritage.org/international-economies/commentary/brazils-bolsonaro-should-follow-trumps-lead-and-slash.

Rucker, P., and R. Costa. (2017). "Bannon Vows a Daily Fight for 'Deconstruction of the Administrative State.'" *Washington Post* (February 23), www.washingtonpost.com/politics/top-wh-strategist-vows-a-daily-fight-for-deconstruction-of-the-administrative-state/2017/02/23/03f6b8da-f9ea-11e6-bf01-d47f8cf9b643_story.html.

Ryan, A. (1962). "Locke and the Dictatorship of the Bourgeoisie." *Political Studies*, 13(2): 219–230.

Sandoval, E., and J. D. Goodman. (2022). "'Errors' at Treatment Plant Force 1 Million in Austin to Boil Their Water." *New York Times* (February 7), www.nytimes.com/2022/02/07/us/austin-boil-water.html.

Schwartz, I. (2017). "Spicer On Deep State: No Question Officials From Last 8 Years Would Seek To Continue Obama Agenda." *RealClear Politics* (March 11), www.realclearpolitics.com/video/2017/03/11/spicer_on_deep_state_no_question_officials_from_last_8_years_would_seek_to_continue_obama_agenda.html.

Sherk, J. (2017). "Proposed Labor Reforms." https://assets.documentcloud.org/documents/6948593/Sherk-White-House-document.pdf.

Sherk, J. (2022). "Tales From the Swamp: How Federal Bureaucrats Resisted President Trump." America First Policy Institute (February 1), https://amer

icafirstpolicy.com/latest/20222702-federal-bureaucrats-resisted-president-trump.

Sherk, J. (2022a). "Deeply Partisan Federal Bureaucrats Selectively Enforce The Laws, Eliminating Equal Justice For All." *The Federalist* (March 30), https://thefederalist.com/2022/03/30/deeply-partisan-federal-bureaucrats-selectively-enforce-the-laws-eliminating-equal-justice-for-all/.

Sherk, J. (2022b). "The President Needs the Power to Fire Bureaucrats." *Wall Street Journal* (August 9), www.wsj.com/articles/the-power-to-fire-insubordinate-bureaucrats-schedule-f-executive-order-trump-deborah-birx-at-will-civil-service-removal-appeals-11659989383.

Sherk, J. (2023). "Forum on Schedule F and the Future of the Public Service." (Jun2 29). Washington: National Academy of Public Administration,www.youtube.com/watch?v=wSUY9ito9TM

Simmons, A. J. (1992). *The Lockean Theory of Rights*. Princeton: Princeton University Press.

Singhvi, A. M. (2014). "An End to the Spoils System." *The Times of India* (July 4), https://timesofindia.indiatimes.com/blogs/candid-corner/an-end-to-the-spoils-system/.

Smith, A. (1776). *An Inquiry into the Nature and Causes of the Wealth of Nations*. London: W. Strahan.

Society for Human Resource Management and Willis Towers Watson (2020). *The Future Chief People Officer: Imagine. Invent. Ignite. Why Empowered HR Leaders Are Key to Capturing Growth in the New World of Work*, www.shrm.org/hr-today/trends-and-forecasting/research-and-surveys/documents/future%20chief%20people%20officer-imagine.%20invent.%20ignite.%20final.pdf.

Stanley, M. (n.d.). "Civil Service History." www.civilservant.org.uk/misc-history.html.

Stein, H. (1994). "Remembering Adam Smith." *Wall Street Journal Asia* (April 7), 8.

Stephen Skowronek, S. (1982). *Building A New American State: The Expansion of National Administrative Capacities, 1877-1920*. Cambridge: Cambridge University Press.

Suetonius (2007). *The Twelve Caesars*, trans. R. Graves. London: Penguin Classics.

Svara, J. H. (1985). "Dichotomy and Duality: Reconceptualizing the Relationship between Policy and Administration in Council-Manager Cities." *Public Administration Review*, 45 (January/February), 221–232.

Tuckness, A. (2020). "Locke's Political Philosophy." In E. N. Zala, ed., *The Stanford Encyclopedia of Philosophy* (Winter), https://plato.stanford.edu/archives/win2020/entries/locke-political/.

Tully, J. (1980). *A Discourse on Property: John Locke and His Adversaries.* Cambridge: Cambridge University Press.

UK Tea and Infusions Association (2023). "Frequently Asked Questions about Tea." www.tea.co.uk/tea-faqs.

US Bureau of Labor Statistics (2023). "Union Members – 2022" (January 19), www.bls.gov/news.release/union2.nr0.htm.

US Department of Commerce, Office of Inspector General (2020). *Evaluation of NOAA's*

September 6, 2019, Statement About Hurricane Dorian Forecasts, Final Report No. OIG-20-032-I (June 26), www.oig.doc.gov/OIGPublications/OIG-20-032-I.pdf.

US Executive Office of the President (2021). "Fact Sheet: Executive Order Establishing the White House Task Force on Worker Organizing and Empowerment" (April 26), www.whitehouse.gov/briefing-room/statements-releases/2021/04/26/fact-sheet-executive-order-establishing-the-white-house-task-force-on-worker-organizing-and-empowerment/.

US Government Accountability Office (2016). *Federal Hiring: OPM Needs to Improve Management and Oversight of Hiring Authorities*, GAO-16-521 (September 1), www.gao.gov/products/gao-16-521.

US Government Accountability Office (2020a). *Veteran Federal Employment: OPM and Agencies Could Better Leverage Data to Help Improve Veteran Retention Rates*, GAO-20-592. (July 22), www.gao.gov/products/gao-20-592.

US Government Accountability Office (2020b). *DHS Service Contracts: Increased Oversight Needed to Reduce the Risk Associated with Contractors Performing Certain Functions*, GAO-20-417 (May 7), www.gao.gov/products/gao-20-417.

US Merit Systems Protection Board (2020). *The Merit System Principles: Keys to Managing the Federal Workforce*, www.mspb.gov/studies/studies/The_Merit_System_Principles_Keys_to_Managing_the_Federal_Workforce_1371890.pdf.

US Office of Personnel Management (2003). *Biography of an Ideal: A History of the Federal Civil Service*. Washington, DC: US Government Printing Office.

US Office of Personnel Management (2022). *Employment of Veterans in the Federal Executive Branch: Fiscal Year 2020* (May). www.fedshirevets.gov/

veterans-council/veteran-employment-data/employment-of-veterans-in-the-federal-executive-branch-fy2020.pdf.

US Office of Personnel Management (n.d.). "Policy, Data, Oversight: Veterans Services," www.opm.gov/policy-data-oversight/veterans-services/vet-guide-for-hr-professionals/

Van Riper, P. P. (1958). *History of the United States Civil Service*. Evanston, IL: Row, Peterson.

Viner, J. (1927). "Adam Smith and Laissez-faire." *The Journal of Political Economy*. 35:2 (April), 198–232.

Voltaire (1764). *Voltaire's Philosophical Dictionary*, www.gutenberg.org/files/18569/18569-h/18569-h.htm.

Wagner, E. (2020). "As White House Steps Up Schedule F Implementation, 'Lawmakers Don't Get It.'" *GovExec* (December 14), www.govexec.com/management/2020/12/white-house-steps-schedule-f-implementation-lawmakers-dont-get-it/170722/.

Wakefield, D. (1961). "William F. Buckley, Jr.: Portrait of a Complainer." *Esquire* (January), 50.

Waldo, D. (1948). *The Administrative State: A Study of the Political Theory of American Public Administration*. New York: Ronald Press. 65.

Waldo, D. (1984). "The Perdurability of the Politics-Administration Dichotomy: Woodrow Wilson and the Identity Crisis in Public Administration." In J. Rabin and J. S. Bowman, eds., *Politics and Administration*. New York: Marcel Dekker, 219–233.

Water Science School (2018). "Aqueducts Moe Water In the Past and Today." Washington: US Geological Survey (June 5), www.usgs.gov/special-topics/water-science-school/science/aqueducts-move-water-past-and-today.

Weber, M. (1947). *The Theory of Social and Economic Organizations*. London: Free Press of Glencoe, Collier-Macmillan.

Wei, J. C., and A. Winroth. (2022). *Medieval Canon Law: Introduction*. Cambridge: Cambridge University Press, www.cambridge.org/core/books/abs/cambridge-history-of-medieval-canon-law/medieval-canon-law-introduction/B5DD73317FF615F2E6D98F5AA938F35A.

White House (2020). "Andrew Jackson." https://obamawhitehouse.archives.gov/1600/presidents/andrewjackson.

White, L. D. (1958). *The Republican Era: 1869-1901*. New York: Macmillan.

Wildavsky, A. (2018). *The Art and Craft of Policy Analysis*, ed. B.G. Peters. London: Palgrave Macmillan.

Wilson, W. (1887). "The Study of Administration." *Political Science Quarterly* 2:2 (June), 187–222.

Worth, R. F. (2017). *A Rage for Order: The Middle East in Turmoil, From Tahir Square to Isis*. New York: Farrar, Straus and Giroux.

Wu, C., and R. Wilkes. (2018). "Local-National Political Trust Patterns: Why China Is an Exception." *International Political Science Review*, 39:4, 436–454.

Wyld, D. C. (2022). *The Age of Remote Work: How COVID-19 Transformed Organizations in Real Time*. Washington, DC: IBM Center for the Business of Government, www.businessofgovernment.org/sites/default/files/How%20COVID-19%20Transformed%20Organizations%20in%20Real%20Time_0.pdf.

Yang, S. (2016). "Exploring Wisdom in the Confucian Tradition: Wisdom as Manifested by Fan Zhongyan." *New Ideas in Psychology* 41, 1–7.

Zhou, X. (2021). *Chinese Bureaucracy through Three Lenses: Weberian, Confucian, and Marchian*. Cambridge: Cambridge University Press.

Zimmerman, M. (2020). "QAnon's Rise in Japan Shows the Conspiracy Theory's Global Spread," *The Print* (November 30), https://theprint.in/world/qanons-rise-in-japan-shows-the-conspiracy-theorys-global-spread/554698/

Acknowledgments

In a book with this long a sweep of history, any author is lucky to build on the foundations laid by generations of scholars. In fact, much of what I wanted to do in writing this book was to examine the threads of expertise as they have been woven into government over the last two thousand years. I'm deeply indebted to the many researchers who have explored this issue over the ages.

I'm especially grateful to truly inspirational public administration scholars who staked out the territory in the modern era. Luther Gulick superbly crystallized the fundamentals of public administrative theory. My dissertation adviser, James W. Fesler, had a keen eye for tracking the big pictures of today back to their ancient roots. Indeed, he taught me about the enduring questions of ancient times to which the leaders of today seek new answers. During my days at the University of Virginia, Frederick C. Mosher endlessly entertained me with his stories about the twists and turns of administrative practice—and he shone a bright light on the challenges of democracy in the public service.

A distinguished student of canon law, Rev. Jimmy Hsu, CSP, guided me through the evolution of the rule of law during the Dark Ages and, in particular, helped me discover why they were not quite so dark after all. And my great friend and muse, John DiIulio, has long provided inspiration on the role of leadership in the service of the public.

Finally, I remain eternally grateful to my wife Sue, whose support has always been remarkable and whose vision of what is truly important and fundamental has been an unshakable keystone during our nearly 50 years of marriage.

Cambridge Elements ☰

Public and Nonprofit Administration

Andrew Whitford

University of Georgia

Andrew Whitford is Alexander M. Crenshaw Professor of Public Policy in the School of Public and International Affairs at the University of Georgia. His research centers on strategy and innovation in public policy and organization studies.

Robert Christensen

Brigham Young University

Robert Christensen is professor and George Romney Research Fellow in the Marriott School at Brigham Young University. His research focuses on prosocial and antisocial behaviors and attitudes in public and nonprofit organizations.

About the Series

The foundation of this series are cutting-edge contributions on emerging topics and definitive reviews of keystone topics in public and nonprofit administration, especially those that lack longer treatment in textbook or other formats. Among keystone topics of interest for scholars and practitioners of public and nonprofit administration, it covers public management, public budgeting and finance, nonprofit studies, and the interstitial space between the public and nonprofit sectors, along with theoretical and methodological contributions, including quantitative, qualitative and mixed-methods pieces.

The Public Management Research Association

The Public Management Research Association improves public governance by advancing research on public organizations, strengthening links among interdisciplinary scholars, and furthering professional and academic opportunities in public management.

Cambridge Elements ≡

Public and Nonprofit Administration

Elements in the Series

Critical Race Theory: Exploring Its Application to Public Administration
Norma M. Riccucci

Rage Giving
Jennifer A. Taylor and Katrina Miller-Stevens

Apples to Apples: A Taxonomy of Networks in Public Management and Policy
Branda Nowell and H. Brinton Milward

Country Size and Public Administration
Marlene Jugl

Contingent Collaboration: When to Use Which Models for Joined-up Government
Rodney J. Scott and Eleanor R. K. Merton

*The Hidden Tier of Social Services: Frontline Workers' Provision of Informal
Resources in the Public, Nonprofit, and Private Sectors*
Einat Lavee

Networks in the Public Sector: A Multilevel Framework and Systematic Review
Michael D. Siciliano, Weijie Wang, Qian Hu, Alejandra Medina
and David Krackhardt

Organizing and Institutionalizing Local Sustainability: A Design Approach
Aaron Deslatte

*When Governments Lobby Governments: The Institutional Origins of
Intergovernmental Persuasion in America*
Youlang Zhang

Public Administration and Democracy: The Complementarity Principle
Anthony M. Bertelli and Lindsey J. Schwartz

Redefining Development: Resolving Complex Challenges in a Global Context
Jessica Kritz

Experts in Government: The Deep State from Caligula to Trump and Beyond
Donald F. Kettl

A full series listing is available at: www.cambridge.org/EPNP

Printed in the United States
by Baker & Taylor Publisher Services